# EASY DOG FOOD RECIPES

# *Easy*
# DOG
# FOOD
## RECIPES

### 60 Healthy Dishes to Feed Your Pet Safely

**Scott Shanahan**

callisto
publishing
an imprint of Sourcebooks

*I would like to dedicate this book to my daughter, Delilah, whose love for animals inspires me every day to strive toward helping animals have the best life possible.*

Published by Callisto Publishing LLC C/O Sourcebooks LLC

P.O. Box 4410, Naperville, Illinois 60567-4410

(630) 961-3900

callistopublishing.com

Printed and bound in China

OGP 2

# CONTENTS

# INTRODUCTION

Hi, my name is Scott. Welcome to a new world of pet care, where cooking healthy meals for your dog has the potential to show you a whole new side of your dog.

I owned and operated a pet care company in Los Angeles for 15 years and had an average of 50 clients at any given time. These clients came to me with food questions and concerns, as well as for advice on the best care for their furry family member, including late-night panic over something their pup had eaten. I also had good relationships with veterinarians, whom I consulted on tips for feeding, health needs, and general pet care.

Food was always a crucial part of my home pet care routine, but I really started paying attention to what I was feeding my own sweet Maddie and Sophie, a hound mix and a shepherd, respectively, as they entered the final stages of their lives. It became very important to ensure their meals enhanced their quality of life.

It was Maddie who started to show clear signs that she wasn't getting the nutrition she needed. I started researching canine eating habits and looking closer into manufactured food, including the formulas and labels on the packages. I wasn't happy with what I learned. So, I consulted a veterinarian colleague, and I started making semidried food for Maddie, focusing on providing the essential nutrients that were easily absorbed by her failing liver. Maddie went from having no appetite to eating again a couple of times a day. These were extreme circumstances, but seeing firsthand the big difference those changes made in the dog had me hooked on homemade food.

Then there's Sophie's story. Several years later, our old dog was diagnosed with hemangiosarcoma and given two weeks to live. Hemangiosarcoma is a very aggressive cancer, with masses in tough-to-see places. When the masses show up in X-rays or you see your dog's demeanor has changed, it is often much too late to do anything about it. In Sophie's case, I found a mushroom extract that slowed the growth of the masses, so we enjoyed 13 more months with our lovely hound. The mushroom extract didn't cure Sophie's cancer—food alone cannot do that—but it did improve her quality of life and extend the time between new growths. My vet colleague, Dr. Oh, passed this information on to people in his veterinarian practice, and other families were able to extend the time they had with their pets. That is what this is really all about. It's rare that you find something so helpful in a time of despair, but it occasionally does happen. I am not claiming that any of the recipes given here are miracles, but if you feed your dog healthy, fresh ingredients every day, it's certainly not going to hurt.

Manufactured food is cause for concern in several areas. Over the years, I have seen dogs form allergies from eating the same kibble for too long, where their skin is so dry that they scratch themselves raw and create bald spots, kind of the opposite of a hot spot. Trying to track down which ingredient might be the culprit can feel like chasing your tail. Food recalls are another issue. Recalls are often not mainstream news; you have to keep up through your own diligence, and then you are often left checking serial numbers and dates nervously, waiting for new alerts, not knowing if you've fed dangerous ingredients to your dog. And to top it all off, you have to change your dog's food, which can upset your pup's system while you research new companies and formulas.

By the end of this book, you will have a general understanding of what constitutes a balanced meal for your dog and how to change up their meals in a way that is gentle on them and suits your lifestyle. You will also get an idea for what to look out for physically and how to read your dog's body language, so you know when to customize and adapt these recipes to meet both your dog's needs and your cooking routine and lifestyle. All the recipes given are designed with short ingredient lists, easy prep, and quick cook times. If there are a few ingredients in here that you don't particularly like, you'll learn how to substitute those out for other choices that still properly balance the meal. If you love chicken, you'll figure out how to prepare a meal for everyone (dogs and people), and how to pull the dog portions before adjusting the recipe with seasonings you enjoy. You'll learn which ingredients are safe for humans and toxic for dogs. Some foods are healthy for you, but not for your pup.

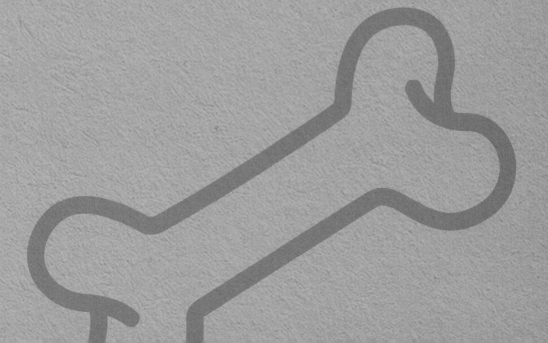

# HOW TO USE THIS BOOK

Chapter 1 is about the benefits of cooking homemade meals for your dog, including how to determine from your dog's physical reactions what they need and when to cut back. You'll learn to watch your dog's behavior—high energy or lethargy—to see if they are overeating or if you need to bulk up their portions a bit. You will also learn how to read dog food labels in this section of the book.

In chapter 2, we'll talk about the canine's nutritional needs and how these recipes are designed to meet them. Some of the ingredients overlap to help keep the ingredients lists short and ease transitioning through a rotating feeding schedule. By slowly adding different foods, you can ensure your dog's body can absorb the nutrients evenly.

Chapter 3 helps you set up your kitchen with all the necessary gear needed for these recipes. Don't worry, you probably already have the necessary tools, but we'll go over that in this chapter. This chapter will also outline how much food to feed your dog, depending on size and age. You will also learn the best way to transition your dog from store-bought food to tasty homemade meals.

The 60 recipes in this book call for natural, whole foods whenever available, so what's safe for your dog is also safe for you to eat. You'll find an array of recipes for treats, main dishes, saucy extras, and tasty sides in chapters 4 through 7 that you can make for your dog, trying out different meals to see what really pleases your pooch. In chapter 8, I've taken a few of the recipes and added some extra steps so you can make dinner for your dog *and* for yourself. Just be careful that you add only the extra ingredients meant for people after you've portioned the canine serving. Most of all, have fun experimenting with these recipes while learning to cook for your dog.

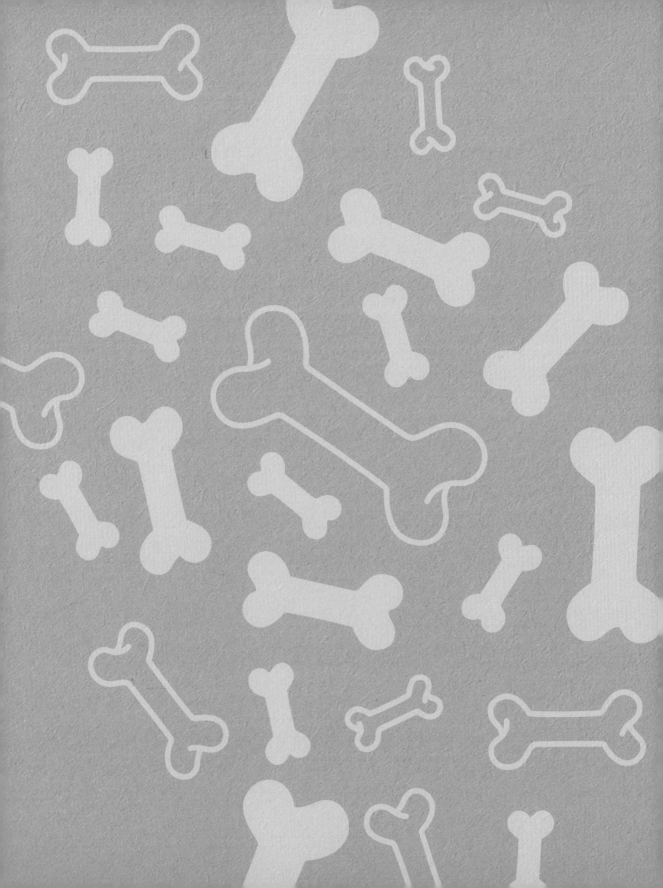

# Part One

## YOUR DOG'S DIET AND HEALTH

For thousands of years, dogs and humans have worked together—from wolves scavenging scraps alongside hunters to guide dogs helping people with disabilities and everything in between. Nowadays, most of us think of our dogs as part of the family. They are our best friends. We all want what's best for our dogs, and we want their life to be the best it can possibly be. We love our relationships with our dogs, and cooking for them is an excellent way to bond with your buddy. Dogs appreciate food, and the way they feel comes through in their attitude. I have seen many dogs become so much more expressive with an exciting diet change. They know when it's dinnertime, and when they're excited by the prospect of a meal, they will remind you to feed them in charming ways.

*Chapter One*

# BECOMING A HOME CHEF FOR YOUR DOG

Over the years as a pet care provider, I cared for dozens and dozens of dogs and learned the feeding habits of each individual pup on my roster. I saw firsthand the attitude changes that accompanied a diet optimized with vitamins and other nutrients, as well as the lethargy and irritation caused by a diet lacking in something. I've helped clients find the right food and determine allergies from watching dog behavior day in and day out. We all care deeply about our dogs, and cooking their meals at home is one way to show them. As a bonus, we get to reap the benefits ourselves.

## Homemade Dog Food

Think about your own diet. There are certain foods or recipes you might eat regularly, but you mix it up to avoid boredom and malnutrition. For example, food like beef jerky is delicious, but would you want to eat it for every meal? Store-bought dry dog food is dehydrated, baked, and condensed, which removes all the moisture content. Sound familiar? It's essentially the same process as drying out beef jerky.

Dried mainstream dog food offers a longer shelf life, but the methods used to produce huge batches of food remove many vital nutrients from the original ingredients. To make up for this loss of nutrients, pet food brands add powdered supplements to the food. These additions ensure the companies still hit the federally mandated minimum requirements necessary to claim their food is a complete and balanced meal for your dog.

Do you know what your dog is eating? By cooking for your dog, you know every single ingredient going into their body. This makes it easier to spot something that may not be agreeing with them and adjust ingredients for their unique nutritional needs. Mass-produced dog food tends to have a staggering list of ingredients, including preservatives, so it can be hard to tell precisely which ones are helping your dog and which ones are harming them.

Now that you've decided to become a home chef for your dog, there will be no more running out of dog food and having to run out to the pet store before they close. You'll still have to get groceries, but chances are you're doing that anyway. Another huge bonus? Cooking the fresh and frozen ingredients in these recipes will add a good deal of moisture to your dog's meals. This is a great way to make sure your buddy is getting all the water they need every day. Dogs can stop short of hydrating sufficiently. On days with big hikes, hot days, or highly active days, your dog is probably at the water bowl frequently. These days aside, the average dog sleeps 12 to 14 hours a day, so trips to the watering hole might not happen as much as they should be.

Pets are part of the family for most people, and it is often a priority to create the best life possible for our furry friends. Home-cooked meals are just another way to give them what's best. Don't worry if cooking for your dog sounds like a lot of time and effort. Just like preparing meals for yourself or your family, you'll fall into a rhythm quickly and be able to whip up simple recipes without a ton of effort. Once you determine which ingredients are supercharging your pup, you can adapt other recipes in the book to include impactful ingredients. The recipes are designed to give you the freedom to fit cooking for your dog into your life in the manner best for you.

## The Many Benefits of DIY

Having complete control over what's going into your dog's body can be an eye-opening experience, and being able to see the changes a fresh diet can make may even lead you to take better care of yourself.

### FRESH AND HEALTHY INGREDIENTS

Most of us are generally aware that fresh and nutrient-rich ingredients are the key to a healthy eating regime. For anyone. You wouldn't put diesel fuel in a race car and expect the same speed and performance as it would get with the high-octane fuel it was built to run on. That's true for the fuel we put into our dogs, too. Each breed, mix, and individual is unique, and each dog's lifestyle is also unique. Taking the time to ensure they have the nutrients their bodies were built to process benefits everything from their energy level to their bladder and immune system function.

### NO FILLERS, WEIRD PROCESSING OF ANIMAL PARTS, OR ADDED DYES

Manufactured dog food has come a long way in the last decade. Some of the things people have paid money for as pet food over the years would send chills down your

## Training Tip for Mealtime Behavior

Over the years, I have cared for many dogs besides mine, and they were often boarded in my home for long periods. I've fed dogs of all temperaments, each with their own baggage around mealtime.

No matter the dog or the diet, there is always one constant to follow: DO NOT encourage any begging from your buddy while you're cooking their meals. No matter how bright or well-trained a dog is, they will not know when you are cooking for them or for yourself. Once you let them cross that line, they'll be in the kitchen with you all the time. Let's face it, tripping hazards while cooking is a recipe for disaster. Pun intended.

Keeping them out of the kitchen during prep and cooking means not feeding them from the stove and, in a best-case scenario, not allowing them in the kitchen when food is being prepared AT ALL. Instead, designate a place for them to eat outside of the kitchen. Visible guidelines are great for dogs, so if you live in a small or open space or aren't a fan of dog gates, create your own boundaries. Kitchen thresholds, rugs, towels, dog beds, and even masking tape can help train your pooch to know where they should wait for dinner.

spine: rotten meat, plastics, and Styrofoam, for example. But there are still plenty of unsavory ingredients going into today's store-bought canine formulas. When manufacturing dog food, companies are held to a lower set of rules and standards than those that our own food must meet. These are known as "feed grade" standards, which are deemed suitable for animals but not humans. These guidelines and regulations allow for some nasty ingredients, such as fillers, processed animal parts, and dyes, to slip through the cracks.

### CONTROL FOR FOOD ALLERGIES

A huge advantage to making your dog food yourself is being able to see how different ingredients affect your dog. If you notice the dog is more energetic after a certain kind of protein, veggie, or other ingredient, you can adapt the recipes around that food choice. Alternatively, if you notice something is slowing the dog down or the food does not seem to be the fuel they need, you can cut it out and adapt the recipes away from that particular ingredient. Cooking meals for your dog can also help control allergies and allows you to make small changes in their diet. This control can help keep the dog from forming new allergies. If a dog gets the exact same meal every day, the chances of developing allergies to that meal increase, and because many manufactured foods are similar in formula, the allergen could be present in many store-bought choices.

### IMPROVED SKIN, COAT, AND OVERALL HEALTH

When dogs get a properly balanced diet, you can see it all over them. Different ingredients are suitable for different things. For example, adding the right amount of omega-3 fatty acids and omega-6 fatty acids is good for a dog's joints and shows in their silky coat. The proper ratio is about four parts omega-6s to one part omega-3s. Eggs are also beneficial to their coat. A proper dose of fatty acids, along with added exercise, typically improves joint health, bones, coats, and muscle growth.

### VARIETY OF MEALS

Everyone enjoys and benefits from a little variety in their diet, but when it comes to your pup, a proper transition time is important. If done too abruptly, changes in your dog's diet can result in gas, diarrhea, or an upset stomach. In my view, the benefits of variety outweigh the difficulty of transitioning between foods. All it takes is a little bit of forethought to switch foods with little to no abdominal discomfort to your dog. (See page 32 for more on transitioning methods.)

The recipes in this book lend themselves to easy food transitions, as they are designed so that you can make small substitutions while cooking them. For example, use ground turkey in a ground beef recipe for a day or two before switching over to a week or two of turkey recipes. This process will allow the dog to easily digest the bulk of the ingredients they've grown accustomed to eating, and they will only have to form new bacteria to digest the protein change. Small changes always give the body a better chance at adapting to the change.

### YOUR DOG'S JOY

Your dog is going to love this new diet. They can smell and taste every ingredient. Separately. You don't have to set their bowl up to look like a three-course meal. If you mix ingredients all together, the dog's senses are advanced enough to enjoy each different flavor.

### HOMEMADE IS BUDGET FRIENDLY

If your dog has an allergy, you can spend vast amounts of time researching foods and testing different ingredients, as well as run up huge vet bills. You also have to factor in the cost of buying new dog foods to try. If can start to feel like you are chasing your tail. Home cooking will allow you to stay ahead of potential allergies by rotating your dog's meals. If your dog has an allergy, these recipes will make it easier to determine what they are allergic to, since the list of ingredients is so much shorter.

- The average cost of quality canned dog food is just over $3 per pound.

- The average cost of quality dry dog food ranges between $2 and $3 per pound.

- The average cost of high-quality fresh store-bought dog food is around $6.50 per pound.

The per-pound cost of homemade dog food is going to be around $6 or $7, as well. However, the more you buy, the more you save. If you have the room, you can buy in bulk and get the cost down even lower.

# The Pros and Cons of Commercial Dog Food

There is almost certainly going to be a time when you need to buy store-bought food; it may not be ideal, but it is a reality. This section will help you decode some of the wording commonly found on store-bought food. With this knowledge, you will be better equipped to make a healthy choice and understand which ingredients to add so your dog still gets the nutrients they need.

## What Goes into Commercially Made (Feed-Grade) Dog Food

Commercially made dog food is produced to cover a considerable range of dogs, a "one size fits most" kind of approach, and is made with many different ingredients. This makes narrowing down a single ingredient that your dog loves, hates, or is allergic to quite tricky. When a dog has an allergic reaction to a food, the owner will often go to a different formula from the same brand. Unfortunately, many formulas share a long list of the same ingredients, so there is no way to determine the allergen. Some common ingredients show up among many different manufacturers, such as by-product meal, cornmeal, meat and bonemeal, soybean meal, and an assortment of artificial flavors and colors. The term *meal*, as it relates to by-products and meat, describes the result of a rendering process that dehydrates meat to remove all the moisture, and then bakes it until it's a powdery substance with a high protein concentration. Unfortunately, it's too good to be true because the base is not made from high-quality meat; instead, manufacturers use the leftovers of slaughtered animals, such as organs, blood, and bone, that are not graded for human consumption.

There are requirements for dog food, including minimum and maximum amounts of some ingredients and vitamin and mineral content. If a formula does not meet nutrient standards on its own, companies often enrich the dog food with synthetic vitamins or minerals. Manufactured dog food also follows food trends that appeal to consumers. For example, many people are jumping on the grain-free bandwagon for their dogs even though there is little (if any) scientific research that shows conclusive benefits to this diet (unless your dog has an allergy to a specific grain). These flexible guidelines leave lots of room for customization and for improvement.

## How to Read a Dog Food Label

Dog food labels can be tricky to read at times. So, we'll start with the basics. At first glance, you will see the food name, weight or count of the contents, and a recipe name. Most dog foods have descriptive names that tell you a little bit about the recipe, such as Chicken Dinner for Dogs, Beef and Potatoes, or Pacific Fish Formula.

You can then move on to the nutritional label and ingredient list. Per the American Kennel Club (AKC) and the Association of American Feed Control Officials (AAFCO), four rules must be followed in production:

1. The 95 percent rule: For a limited ingredient recipe to be named "Chicken for Dogs" or "Salmon Dog Food," it must contain 95 percent of chicken or salmon, respectively, and water does not count. Foods with multiple main ingredients, such as lamb and beef, must contain 95 percent of these ingredients combined.

2. The 25 percent rule: When a label reads "Chicken Dinner for Dogs" or "Pacific Fish Formula," these recipes must contain 25 percent of the named ingredient. This is not a high percentage, so the manufacturer must add a descriptive disclaimer word, such as *dinner*, *entrée*, or *platter*.

3. The "with" rule. Products that fall below the 25 percent rule must use the word *with* to indicate ingredients. For example, a food named "Dog Food with Chicken and Sweet Potato" needs to contain at least 3 percent chicken and 3 percent sweet potato.

4. The "flavor" rule. When the word *flavor* is used in a dog food name, such as "Chicken Flavor Dog Food," the minimum requirement is "the detection of said flavor." Wow. If that doesn't make your mouth water, I don't know what will. Maybe we can add in some Red Dye No. 40. Yum.

Always look for words like *by-product* and *meal* in the ingredient list, which is a term that generally refers to all the parts of the animal you don't see at your local butcher. These throwaway bits of the animal help manufacturers hit a protein requirement without spending extra money on actual meat. Look out for and avoid foods that contain these ingredients because they are of low-quality. Another ingredient to avoid is color or dye. It has historically been added to dog food for visual appeal, but dogs do not care about that. Why add it? The Center for Science in the Public Interest (CSPI) published a report on the risk of food dyes, including ones found in pet foods and treats. Research shows that various dyes such as Blue No. 2, Red No. 40, Yellow No. 5, and Yellow No. 6 can cause tumors in mice, hypersensitivity, and cancer.

## When You Need to Use Store-Bought Food

There are times when you will need to buy store-bought manufactured dog food. There might be a power outage that makes it difficult to cook or even heat up homemade dog food. Perhaps you're out of town using a dog sitter and don't want to ask that person to go through the same canine cooking routine. Or maybe you're just too tired after a really long day. Don't worry, now that you understand dog food labels better, you can identify the commercial formula that will best supplement your pup's home-cooked diet. In doing so, you'll minimize any gastrointestinal discomfort from changing your dog's food. If the store-bought food isn't perfect, you can toss in a few extra nutritious ingredients (see page 83) to make sure your dog isn't missing out on any vital nutrients.

Sometimes a store-bought product is a more reliable choice, especially if your dog needs a specific vet-recommended diet. If a prescription diet is required, discuss with your vet the essential ingredients and quantities for the condition being treated. If you aren't confident you can produce meals to these specifications, the safest bet is your vet's recommendation. Additionally, sometimes a prescription diet is required when your dog is recovering from surgery or a procedure.

Veterinarians have a wealth of knowledge regarding your dog's particular makeup and well-being. It never hurts to run new diet choices by your vet. Ideally, your vet will be knowledgeable about homemade dog food and guide you to certain ingredients that will be ideal for your dog. Having a trusted veterinarian in your corner takes an enormous weight off your shoulders as a pet owner.

## Wrapping It Up

Now you have essential information on store-bought food, how it's made, what to look out for on the label, and when you may need to use it. The recipes and information in this book should help you tackle this new cooking adventure with confidence. However, if cooking your dog's meals from scratch is just not feasible right now, try to ease into it. You don't have to cook entirely from scratch to improve what your dog is getting from their food. By knowing how to identify a quality food and what nutrients to look for (and stay away from), you can improve your dog's diet while cooking a few meals. Start off by adding extras into your dog's store-bought food and making a few treats. If you have plain chicken breasts for dinner, cook an extra one and add it into your dog's meal. If you have an extra can of sodium-free green beans in the pantry, stir it into your dog's regular food.

You don't have to go all in at once if it seems like too much work or time. However, once you start doing this, you will see it isn't that much extra work, and the benefits are worth it. You won't mind cooking a little more of some things. Fit this change into your lifestyle. If you go to the grocery store every day to cook fresh ingredients, make a little extra every night for your dog and save some for the next morning. If your schedule doesn't allow for daily shopping, make a triple batch of one or two recipes and portion them into individual servings to keep in the freezer for the week.

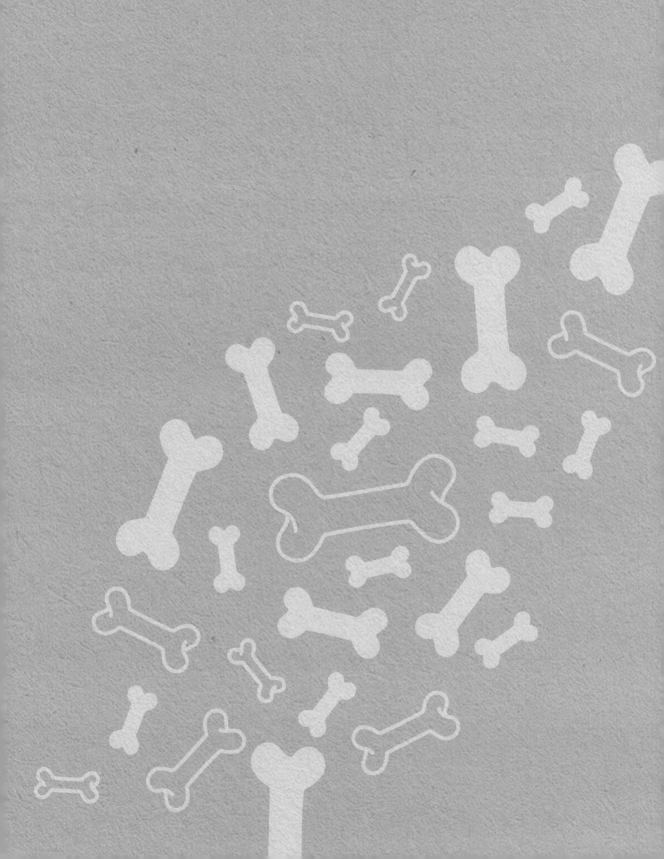

*Chapter Two*

# YOUR DOG'S NUTRITIONAL NEEDS

Your dog's system is a finely tuned, well-oiled machine when given the proper fuel. With a balanced diet, your dog gets all the nutrients needed for their body to do what it is meant to do. All of the vitamins, minerals, fats, proteins, and carbohydrates enter their system and immediately begin to break down to heal, energize, maintain, and replenish their entire system.

## This Diet Is for the Dogs

While they say that presentation is 80 percent of the meal for a person, this is not the case with dogs. They can smell and taste every different ingredient, all at the same time, and don't care if you garnish the bowl. Depending on your dog's size and the ingredients used, you may want to put the entire recipe through a food processor. Other times, just mixing the already diced and cooked ingredients together can be appealing, too.

All of the ingredients used in this book are safe and healthy for dogs to eat, and the recipes are balanced, so you'll see which ingredients really make your buddy thrive. It will also be apparent if something doesn't digest well or falls short of giving the same boost as other ingredients.

The recipes contain essential nutrients such as protein and fats, as well as micronutrients like vitamins and minerals. It can be helpful to know what these components do in your dog's body when considering which recipes to make.

### Protein

When digested, protein breaks down into amino acids. Amino acids are needed to build and repair muscles and other body tissue. They're also needed to form skin cells and grow hair. Amino acids keep the immune system fighting, help the body create hormones and enzymes to help absorb nutrients, and supply energy.

Protein can't be stored by the body, so it is important to feed it to your dog every day. The amount of protein to give your dog will depend on the amount of exercise your dog gets. A working dog will require a very high-protein diet for replenishment, while an adult dog, who may lie around more, won't need as much.

Some of the best proteins are meats—beef, chicken, duck, lamb, seafood, and turkey. Proteins are also found in eggs and some grains and legumes.

There are 22 amino acids at work in your dog's metabolism: 12 that their bodies can create themselves and 10 that need to be derived from their food.

Food is broken down by stomach acids, then the pancreas takes the liquified, broken down food and stomach acid and produces enzymes to help the nutrients be absorbed where they are needed. This helps replenish and repair tired muscles.

## Fats

Fats are the first nutrients to be absorbed by the body for energy. Before protein and carbohydrates, the body burns fat. Fat also plays a part in the body's absorption of vitamins and minerals and the digestion process. Fats are made up of fatty acids, and some fatty acids—the omega-6 and omega-3 fatty acids—can't be produced by a dog's body. That's why it is important to add them into the diet in a ratio of about 4:1 (four parts omega-6s to one part omega-3s).

## Fiber

Fiber is found in many dog-friendly foods, including broccoli, peas, sweet potatoes, carrots, apples, and pumpkin. Some fiber ferments in a dog's digestive tract, turning into fatty acids that help keep bad bacteria away. Others are soluble, working more as a lubricant to aid passage through the intestinal walls. In this way, when eaten regularly, fiber can work to both slow down the digestion process when your dog has diarrhea and speed up the process if they're constipated. Slowing down digestion allows nutrients to be absorbed into the system. Most of the fiber in common fruits and vegetables are the soluble type and help keep the gut healthy, happy, and moving smoothly.

## Carbohydrates

Carbs are split into two groups: simply carbohydrates and complex carbohydrates. Simple carbohydrates require almost no breakdown and are ready for digestion immediately. They don't often have any nutrients to offer; they are immediately turned into glucose and burned for energy. These are fructose, sucrose, and lactose, and they're found in honey.

Complex carbohydrates dietary fibers and starches. They have to be broken down in digestion, making it a slower process. They are still an energy source, and the extra time allows any other nutrients to be absorbed. These are found in grains, potatoes, beans, and some veggies.

Oatmeal, brown rice, millet, and quinoa are all great sources.

## Vitamins

There are two types of vitamins: fat-soluble and water-soluble. Extra fat-soluble vitamins are stored in fat tissue, while unused water-soluble vitamins are flushed from the system.

### FAT-SOLUBLE VITAMINS

* **Vitamin A:** Vitamin A is in carrots and helps with cell function, immune function, fetal development, growth, and vision.

* **Vitamin D:** Vitamin D can be found in salmon, liver, and eggs, and helps balance the absorption of phosphorus and calcium for healthy bone growth. It is crucial in both development and maintenance. However, according to the FDA, extremely high amounts of vitamin D can be fatal. Because it is a fat-soluble vitamin, excess amounts are not filtered out through a dog's urine. Instead, extra vitamin D is stored in fat cells in the liver. Routine vet visits and blood tests will help you gauge exactly where your pet's levels are. Since all dogs are different, your dog's levels may be sufficient or you may still need to add some supplements or cod liver oil to their meals. If you can meet their needs with food, rather than supplements, I always encourage that.

* **Vitamin E:** Salmon, eggs, and spinach contain vitamin E. It helps cell function and growth and supports a healthy immune system. According to Dr. Jennifer Coates, author of the *Dictionary of Veterinary Terms: Vet-Speak Deciphered for the Non-Veterinarian*, vitamin E is a potent antioxidant that can help prevent heart disease and arthritis.

* **Vitamin K:** According to the American Kennel Club, vitamin K is instrumental in activating blood clotting in your dog. It is generally found in leafy greens. Ingestion of certain rat and mouse poisons inhibit dogs' ability to use vitamin K in their bodies, which leads to hemorrhaging and death if not treated.

- **B vitamins:** These include biotin, folate (or folic acid), niacin, pantothenic acid, riboflavin, thiamine, vitamin $B_6$, and vitamin $B_{12}$. These serve a wide variety of purposes including energy maintenance, neural pathway development, and enzyme and immunity boosts. B vitamins can be found in brown rice, green beans, and legumes.

- **Vitamin C:** Found in blueberries, cranberries, and watermelon, for example, vitamin C helps stave off free radicals, delays cognitive decline, and reduces inflammation.

- **Choline:** Choline is found in eggs, liver, fish, and meats. Choline chloride is a salt that forms naturally and supports your dog's brain and liver functions.

## Minerals

Minerals are an important piece of a balanced meal. They often aren't needed in large quantities, but they all work together, activating one another to keep everything functioning properly.

### MACROMINERALS

These are found in larger quantities in the body.

- **Calcium:** Calcium is found in broccoli, spinach, legumes, and crushed egg shells, and it supports healthy bones and teeth.

- **Phosphorus:** Phosphorus is found in most proteins, and it helps keep kidneys healthy. Along with calcium, it's important for maintaining strong bones and teeth.

- **Magnesium:** Magnesium is found in legumes, whole grains, and some fatty fish, and it helps keep muscles healthy.

- **Sodium:** Sodium is found in many proteins. At a low level, sodium helps support cell functions, including nerve signal transmission.

- **Chloride:** Chloride works with the sodium, and it helps dogs create hydrochloric acid in the stomach.

- **Potassium:** Potassium is found in bananas, potatoes, beans, and peas. It is a key part of a maintaining healthy electrical functions, such as those electrical charges in the nerves, heart, and muscles. It also supports bone density.

* **Sulfur:** Sulfur is found in eggs, and it helps neutralize harmful nitrates in the body.

### TRACE MINERALS

These are needed in much smaller quantities because dogs can produce these trace minerals on their own, but not necessarily enough of them.

* **Iron:** Iron is found in lean meats, salmon, and sardines. It helps the body create healthy, oxygenated red blood cells.

* **Zinc:** Fish is a great source for zinc, which helps heal wounds. It's also an important part of protein and carbohydrate metabolism.

* **Copper:** Copper is found in meat, liver, fish, whole grains, and legumes. It helps the body absorb iron and helps the formation of connective tissue.

* **Chromium:** Chromium is found in beef and poultry and many fruits and veggies. It helps support the cellular uptake of glucose, meaning it helps the body turn carbs into energy.

* **Iodine:** Found in shrimp, cod, tuna, and grains, iodine helps the thyroid gland function properly.

* **Selenium:** Found in fish, meat, poultry, and grains, selenium helps immune function and thyroid hormone metabolism.

* **Manganese:** Found in green veggies, fruits, whole grains, and legumes, manganese supports enzyme and neurological functions.

# What Not to Feed Your Dog

Knowing which ingredients to avoid can be the most daunting part of cooking for your dog. Some ingredients that are safe and nutritious for people are absolutely toxic to dogs. Some are well known, but others are more obscure.

Chocolate is a good example of a well-known toxin—everybody seems to know to not give chocolate to a dog. Grapes (and raisins) are another well-known example of an item not safe for dogs, but what we learn about nutrition and dogs is always evolving, and sometimes that means ruling out old information without new information to replace it. Conventional knowledge used to pin the problem with grapes on the dog's digestive system: it was simply unable to break down the grape's skin. That theory has been debunked, but we still don't know why grapes are bad for dogs. Let's take a closer look at the toxic foods you should never feed your dog.

## Alcohol

Your dog's consumption of alcohol can very quickly lead to alcohol poisoning. Signs of this include depression or lethargy, incoordination, drooling, vomiting or retching, weakness, collapse, decreased respiratory rate, hypoglycemia (low blood sugar), hypotension (low blood pressure), and hypothermia (low body temperature).

## Avocado

Avocados contain persin, which is a fungicidal toxin. It is in the fruit, pits, and leaves of the plant, so no part is safe for your buddy. Signs of avocado poisoning include vomiting, diarrhea, abdominal pain, and difficulty producing stools.

## Caffeine

Caffeine can cause toxicosis in your pooch. According to the Pet Poison Helpline, within one to two hours of ingesting even small amounts of caffeine, dogs will become antsy and can experience hyperactivity, elevated heart rates, tremors, and seizures. Serious cases of poisoning can lead to high temperatures, high blood pressure, collapse, and death.

## Chocolate

Chocolate contains theobromine (and often caffeine), which dogs can't metabolize or can't metabolize efficiently. Symptoms of chocolate poisoning can include diarrhea and vomiting. In more severe cases, sometimes associated with the consumption of dark chocolate or baking chocolate, you may see tremors, seizures, and possibly death. If the sugar content of the chocolate is high, there is also a risk of pancreatitis.

## Grapes and Raisins

Eating grapes and raisins can lead to kidney failure. Vomiting and/or diarrhea will often occur within a few hours of ingestion, and you'll most likely be able to identify the culprit in your dog's vomit or stool. Watch for signs of unusual quietness, lethargy, and loss of appetite followed by difficulty urinating. Other signs of poisoning include unusual bad breath, sores in the mouth, and seizures.

## Kale

Kale contains a salt crystal known as calcium oxalate, which can cause bladder and kidney stones. Dogs with kidney stones might urinate often while producing little urine each time.

## Macadamia Nuts

Eating macadamia nuts can cause weakness in your dog's hindquarters, vomiting, and diarrhea. You may also see that they are shaking constantly, have a high fever, or have lost the ability to walk.

## Milk (Dairy)

Although dogs start out drinking their mother's milk, some develop an intolerance to lactose found in dairy products as they mature. Dairy (including cheese) can cause intestinal distress, discomfort, gas, and diarrhea, simply because many dogs have a difficult time digesting it. Some dogs, however, have no problem digesting dairy.

## Onions, Garlic, and Chives

Onions, garlic, and chives can cause anemia and can very quickly damage red blood cells, resulting in the cells not being able to carry oxygen throughout the body, which can result in organ failure. Onions, in my opinion, seem to be the least talked about toxic food, especially when you consider they can very quickly become fatal. This may be solely because of volume. So many human foods contain large amounts of onions, it may not be easy to identify onions as the root cause of your dog's illness. Look for signs of lethargy, reduced muscle coordination, drooling, a lightening of the gums, dark urine, loose stools, and vomiting.

## Raw Meat, Fish, and Eggs

The simplest reason against feeding raw ingredients to your dog is that they are susceptible to salmonella, *E. coli*, and listeria. And not just for them! Your dog is very likely to wipe his face on the rug or a piece of furniture, and this leaves a chance for salmonella or other bacteria to be lingering around and possibly picked up and spread to other family members.

Fish can carry a nasty parasite that causes "salmon poisoning disease"—although it's not limited to salmon only. Watch for swollen lymph nodes, tiredness, vomiting, diarrhea, and dehydration, and call your vet immediately. It's a treatable, but unpleasant, condition. Dogs can develop a biotin deficiency from raw egg whites after prolonged feeding—it doesn't occur in every dog, but it's safer (and a little kinder) to avoid the risk altogether.

## Salt

Too much salt can cause vomiting, diarrhea, dehydration, seizures, and even comas.

## Xylitol

Xylitol, an artificial sweetener used in lots of people food, is a strong stimulator of insulin release in dogs and can cause a dangerous drop in blood sugar. Xylitol poisoning symptoms appear quickly, usually within 15 to 30 minutes of consumption. Watch for signs of hypoglycemia: vomiting, diminished muscle coordination, lethargy, seizures, and muscle tremors. If untreated, xylitol poisoning can lead to liver failure. It's a common ingredient in sugar-free candies, mints, mouthwashes, and toothpastes, and peanut and other nut butters.

## Bones

There are some bones that are not likely to hurt your dog, but because there are so many gray areas of what is and is not safe, I always find it easiest to keep all bones away from my dogs. Even large bones can break into small pieces, and then they're unsafe, too. Better safe than sorry, and there's no need to cause your dogs any pain—or yourself any worry. It's just not worth it. Keep the bones in the broth (see page 97), and make treats in chapter 4 (see page 37) to give them that crunchy texture that can be beneficial to their teeth.

## Wrapping It Up

The proteins, fats, carbohydrates, vitamins, and minerals found in meats and vegetables will provide a balanced and nutritious diet for your dogs. Now that you know all the ingredients in your kitchen to keep out of your dog's meals, the scariest part is over. Stay away from those foods when prepping dog meals, and make sure any dishes containing those foods are kept away from snooping snouts. I have definitely received calls from panicked dog owners late in the evening because their dog pulled an unsuspecting onion casserole off the counter that was never intended for them. This type of incident results in emergency vet visits, possible stomach pumping, or an overnight stay to monitor internals. Because these dishes contain healthy nutrients for us, it doesn't make sense to ban them from the kitchen. Instead, be aware of their presence and make sure to keep them out of pup's reach.

# SETTING UP YOUR KITCHEN

Now we are going to discuss everything you'll need to have in the kitchen. We'll also have charts to help break down all the necessary information for balanced meals and portions.

## Kitchen Tool Kit

You're going to need some basic kitchen tools to cook these recipes, but if you are equipped to cook basic meals for yourself already, you've probably got most of the tools necessary.

### Cutting Board

Cutting boards come in handy for all your cooking, really. I like flexible, colored cutting boards because I can color code to avoid cross contamination (for example, red for meats and green for veggies). They also make transferring chopped food into a pan or a bowl a breeze.

### Fine Mesh Strainer

A fine mesh strainer is perfect for rinsing quinoa or rice and for draining fat from meat. I prefer one that hangs over the sink, which provides a very controlled scenario when pouring scalding water through it into the sink.

### Ice Cube Trays

These are perfect for bite-size frozen treats. I recommend silicone trays, as they make it very easy to remove frozen treats without breaking their form. Silicone trays come in a variety sizes and fun shapes.

## Immersion Blender or Food Processor

I happen to like an immersion blender when it comes to processing food. It's smaller, more versatile, and easier to clean than a food processor. That said, a food processor gets the job done and can be very helpful, especially if you are cooking larger amounts. No need for both; either one will do.

## Kitchen Knives (High Quality)

High-quality kitchen knives make such a huge difference, but they can cost a fortune. However, an entire set isn't the only way to do it—you can build as you go. Get the feel of a weighted, razor-sharp, high-quality knife, and you will start to realize how much effort and time you've been wasting with dull knives.

## Multicookers

I recommend a stockpot that has a steamer basket attachment. These are sometimes called pasta pots or multicookers (not to be confused with pressure cookers or instant pots). This pot allows you to steam veggies over rice. The upside is that any nutrients that tend to cook out of the veggies drip right into the rice. It will also come with a strainer lid for draining pasta, and fewer pots means less cleanup, and that's always good!

## Nested Mixing Bowls

A set of nested mixing bowls is always helpful. They stack neatly into each other for space-saving storage. Get a set with lids, and they can double as storage containers.

## Nonstick Baking Sheets

Many of the treats in chapter 4 (see page 37) require a baking sheet. Size and variety will depend on your needs; any of them will work for baking the dog treats.

## Pots and Pans

A good set of either nonstick or stainless steel pots and pans are an essential item for any kitchen. You will likely use them every day for years. If cared for, they could be the only set you ever buy. There are a lot of different options out there, so if you don't already own a set, find the style that suits you the best.

## Roasting Pan

A roasting pan is nice to have, but there are other baking pans that have racks to keep meat and bones out of drippings and fat, and they will serve the same purpose. Find the size that's right for you.

## Rolling Pin

The treat recipes require making a dough that needs to be rolled flat. There are different materials and styles available—whichever one allows you to roll dough flat is the right choice.

## Stand Mixer or Hand Mixer

All the treat recipes call for a mixer, and even a couple of the main courses use the stand mixer to shred pulled chicken. A hand mixer will work, too, so if that's what you've got, you can make do. A stand mixer is another tool that, if cared for, will last forever. They come in handy for many recipes, and there are attachments to transform it into a machine suitable for various types of specialty cooking.

## Steamer Basket

Steaming vegetables is a good way to keep their nutrients from cooking out. Boiling vegetables tends to remove many of the nutrients, so steaming is a better option. If you have a multicooker, use the attached steamer basket. You can also buy one on its own.

## Stockpot

Stockpots are ideal for large portions: there's plenty of room to simmer a lot of ingredients and keep the splattering or splashing contained in the deep walls. Look for one with a heavy bottom for best results.

## Storage Containers

A set of airtight containers is probably something you already have, since some meals just keep getting better as leftovers. You'll want to have several different sizes of containers to suit your needs.

## Utensils

A wooden spoon, spatula, and rice paddle are all helpful. These are the tools you'll use every time you cook, regardless of what you cook, so these utensils are a must.

# Optional Helpful Items

## Rice Cooker

A rice cooker is a helpful addition to the kitchen if you've got the room. It makes it almost impossible to burn your rice and frees up space on the stovetop. Many of them double as a steamer (but I don't think they're meant to be used at the same time).

## Slow Cooker

Slow cookers are so helpful when it comes to making bone broth. I feel safer leaving a slow cooker on for 16 hours than leaving a pot on the back burner of the stove. It's a tool you won't use every day, but when the task calls for it, it is helpful to have.

## Vacuum Sealer

This is handy for food storage. Freezing single portions is the most efficient way to work, and this will ensure that your food stays fresh. Freeze portions individually, then transfer them to the refrigerator every couple of days to thaw for feeding.

Many of these items are already going to be in your kitchen. The ones that aren't, well, they have so many uses that once you have them, you'll wonder how you ever lived without them.

> If you regularly cook for your dog, a vacuum sealer is a good investment. It enables you to measure out individual servings and freeze them. Bulk-cooking multiple meals over the weekend and storing them in the freezer means you can take out a few meals at a time to thaw. The cooking process then feels like a well-oiled machine and less like you're scrambling to make dinner for even more mouths every day.

# Your Pup's Pantry

Some things to keep in your pup's pantry are the nonperishables that you'll find yourself using in many different recipes. Organization is always nice. If you can neatly line shelves with uniform jars that are always filled with color-coordinated essentials, I envy you. I wish I lived in a magazine spread, but I haven't gotten around to beautifying my pantry yet. For now, I find clear food-storage bins are helpful. They keep things neat, and you can categorize and keep a variety of items in them, rather than in loose bags, boxes, and jars. Labeled bins make it easy to locate the items you're looking for.

## Bone Broth

Boxed bone broth stays for quite a while before it's been opened, and it is often useful to have around. How much you store will depend on how much bone broth you make from the recipes in chapter 7 (see page 97) and store in the freezer.

## Canned Beans and Vegetables

The great thing about canned beans and vegetables is that, while they may be slightly lower in nutrients than fresh vegetables (which is debated), they are sealed right away, locking in most of their nutrients at their peak. Fresh vegetables are at their peak in the first 24 hours after being picked, and within a week, they lose half of their nutrients. Chickpeas, red kidney beans, and green beans are a few types of canned beans to keep on hand.

## Canned Pumpkin Purée

You will see this over and over again in this book. Pumpkin is so helpful for a dog's digestive system that it's always good to have around.

## Canned Tuna

Keep some cans of safely fished white albacore tuna packed in water (not oil). It's probably something you are already stocking, but it is good for the dogs once in a while, too.

## Dried Beans

It's good to keep bags of dried lentils, millet, and red kidney beans in the pantry. They're not going bad anytime soon, and they're a great protein source.

## Rice

The amount of rice you store will really depend on how much space you have. If you have the room, go buy a huge plastic locking bin and a 50-pound bag of white and/or brown rice from your nearest bulk discount store. You will not regret it. Otherwise, buy in the largest quantity that fits your space.

## Steel-Cut Rolled Oats

Steel-cut rolled oats are a super healthy grain to keep on hand.

# In the Refrigerator

## Broth

If you are using boxed broth, refrigerate after opening. It usually keeps for
4 or 5 days.

## Carrots

Fresh carrots are another thing you probably already have in your refrigerator. Large
fresh carrots are fantastic. Filled with nutrients, they add color and flavor to almost
any meal.

## Eggs (Large, Grade AA)

You probably already keep eggs in the refrigerator. If not, buy cage-free, large,
grade AA, brown eggs. They are probably the healthiest, but whatever eggs you
favor, or that fit in your budget, are going to be fine.

## Meat

Meats expire fast—raw chicken is only safe for a day or so in the refrigerator, and red
meats are good for only a few days in the refrigerator.

## Peanut Butter

Many high-quality peanut butters recommend refrigerator storage. Make sure
the peanut butter you buy does not contain xylitol, which is toxic for dogs. Keep
unopened natural peanut butter upside down when storing. That way, when you
have to stir it to mix it all together, you don't have to fight your way through
rock-hard peanut butter to get to the oil.

# In the Freezer

## Chicken Breasts (Boneless and Skinless)

These don't need to be thawed—they can go straight from the freezer into boiling
water in many recipes.

## Meat

The best way to freeze meat is to buy in bulk and separate it into 1-pound or 3-pound packages for freezing. Thaw them in the refrigerator 24 hours before cooking. Meats and poultry will store for up to 1 year in the freezer, and this method allows you to thaw only what you plan to cook, leaving the rest safely sealed and frozen.

## Veggies

Carrots, peas, and green beans are staples in many recipes, so stock up on these. Broccoli and cauliflower show up, too, though not as often. Frozen vegetables lock in nutrients for up to 1 year.

# How Much Should You Feed Your Furry Friend?

The feeding portions you see on packaging are not perfect. Although based on science, they are suggestions, not set in stone. The best way to decide how much to feed your dog is to watch them and adjust accordingly. If a package says your dog should eat 2 cups per day but your dog is overweight, then cut it back a bit. If your dog seems like he is scavenging for food or a little cranky, maybe he is not getting quite enough and needs a more substantial portion. Portion recommendations do not take into consideration how many treats, snacks, or scraps your dog is getting on the side. Too much food will lead to weight gain.

Weight loss or gain in dogs is 80 percent diet and 20 percent exercise. So, use suggested serving sizes as a starting point and watch your dog's waistline and attitude. When a dog is at a healthy weight, you can generally see the last rib or two, there should be no excess weight around the shoulders, and your dog should be playful and even-tempered. Once achieved, the right portion size for your pup should be apparent, and you can apply that amount to all the different meals you're making your dog. If you know one meal is extra filling, feed your dog a little less of that recipe. If you know another meal leaves *you* wanting more, give *them* a little extra. At the end of the day, you will be eating the same meals as your dog, so if your dog weighs half as much as you do, their portion will be about half the size of yours.

# Your Dog's Bowl

A balanced meal for a healthy adult dog is composed of three primary parts: Protein, carbohydrates, and fat.

🐾 Your dog's meal should contain **40 percent protein**, which should be derived mostly from meat and seafood. (In some recipes, other ingredients such as millet will also add to the protein count.)

🐾 The second part will consist of **40 percent carbohydrates** derived from fruits, vegetables, grains, and starches.

🐾 The remaining **20 percent is fat**, derived from actual fat, fatty acids, and oils.

# Portion Control Chart

These feeding portions are suggested daily servings. However, I recommend separating this into two feedings per day: one in the morning and another in the evening.

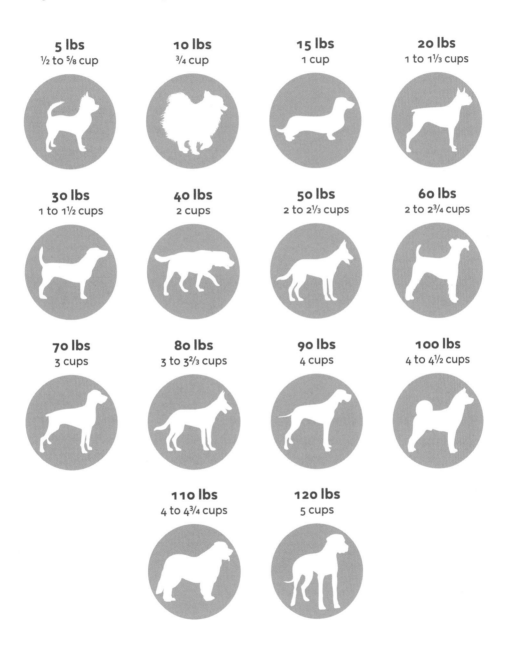

**5 lbs**
½ to ⅝ cup

**10 lbs**
¾ cup

**15 lbs**
1 cup

**20 lbs**
1 to 1⅓ cups

**30 lbs**
1 to 1½ cups

**40 lbs**
2 cups

**50 lbs**
2 to 2⅓ cups

**60 lbs**
2 to 2¾ cups

**70 lbs**
3 cups

**80 lbs**
3 to 3⅔ cups

**90 lbs**
4 cups

**100 lbs**
4 to 4½ cups

**110 lbs**
4 to 4¾ cups

**120 lbs**
5 cups

# Transitioning from Store-Bought Food to Homemade

When transitioning your dog's diet, it's always easiest on their system to do it gradually. If your dog is used to one kind of kibble and you want to switch to homemade, ease into it. Start the process while you've still got half a bag of kibble, and gradually add the new homemade ingredients to the kibble. Start with 30 percent new ingredients and 70 percent kibble, and every few days, change the ratio a bit until you reach 100 percent homemade. If your dog is used to a specific protein, such as chicken, start with the chicken recipes in this book. When rotating recipes for variety, it's good to keep this same practice going. When you switch from one protein to another, use the same veggies or fruits they've had the last few days. Then the dog will be adapting only to the protein change, while the rest of the recipe is less work for their system to digest. Then, when they're adapted to the protein, you can switch up the rest of the ingredients. If you view homemade feeding as a long list of rotating ingredients, it will help you make well-paced changes that keep your dog's system perfectly happy. If your dog was a wild animal, they would follow a similar pattern. They might have the same veggies around their habitat while hunting different types of protein at will.

## Wrapping It Up

Once you get the hang of this, the most efficient way to cook for your dog is by picking a couple of recipes, preparing a batch large enough to supply a week's worth of food, vacuum sealing individual serving portions, and freezing them. To thaw, transfer the portions from the freezer to the refrigerator, one or two meals at a time, and allow the meals to thaw for about 24 hours. Once a month, I suggest rotating a recipe or two, keeping in mind the gradual transition method explained in this chapter.

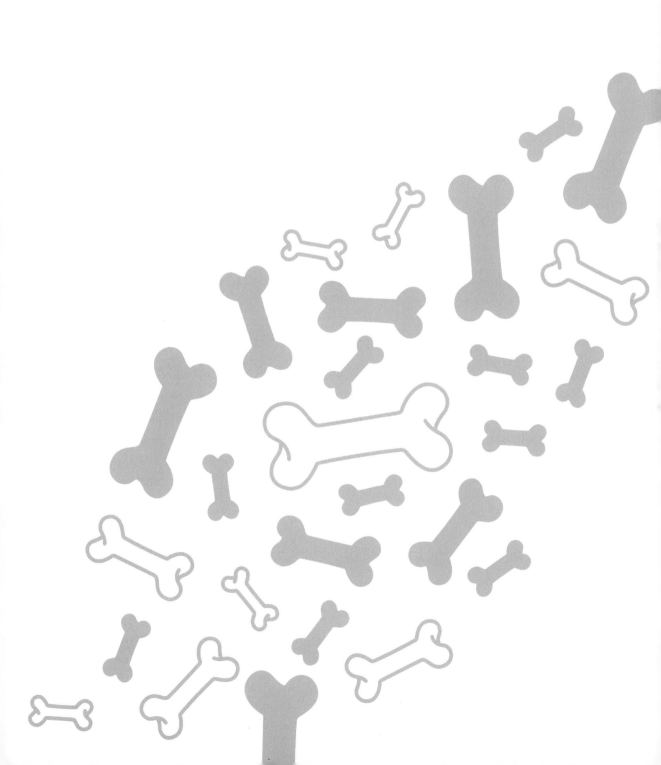

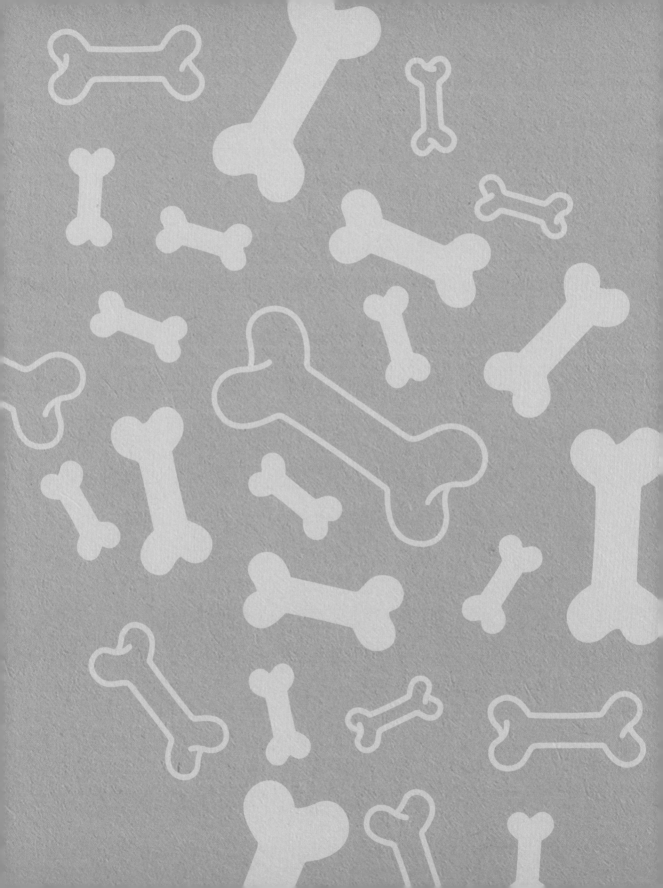

# Part Two

## THE RECIPES

Time to get into the recipes and start cooking! We'll start off with treats—prepping, cooking, storing, and sharing. We'll explore why it's important to change your meal portion size based on how many treats you are giving your dog. Then it's on to the main courses, where you'll find more info on balanced meals, cooking, and feeding schedules. After that, we dive into extra dishes you can cook to bulk up a meal. To finish it off, we've got a chapter dedicated to hanging out and having a meal with your dog.

# Chapter Four

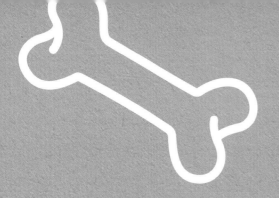

Treats can be a fantastic part of your daily life. Your dog definitely enjoys them! Keep in mind, you should always be aware of the amount of food you're giving your dogs in treat form and adjust their meal portions accordingly. It's easy to lose track, think you've only given a couple of treats, and wind up with an overweight dog. No need for that: You just have to monitor their treat intake.

Treats can be baked longer, left in the cooling oven with the door ajar, or placed on a cooling rack. Many of these methods will create a crunchy treat, and that crunch is rewarding to your dog and can help scrape plaque off their teeth! Treats (if used correctly) can also be helpful for training and are a great energy boost on a long hike.

# CRANBERRY BARS

PREP TIME: 15 MINUTES / COOK TIME: 30 MINUTES

*Sometimes, when you go for a long hike, you can start to feel fatigued before the end of it. Your dog may have the same experience. These bars are a great source of energy for you or your dog, so next time you hit the trail, be sure to bring enough of these bars for both of you.*

**MAKES 15 TO 30 TREATS**

1 cup steel-cut rolled oats

1 cup fresh cranberries

2 large eggs

3 cups whole-wheat flour, divided, plus more for flouring

1. Preheat the oven to 350°F. Line a baking sheet with parchment paper or a silicone baking mat and set aside.

2. In the bowl of an electric mixer fitted with the paddle attachment, beat the oats, cranberries, and eggs on medium-high speed until well mixed, 1 to 2 minutes.

3. Reduce the speed to low and gradually add 2½ cups of flour, beating until just mixed.

4. Beat in the remaining flour, ¼ cup at a time, just until the dough is no longer sticky.

5. Turn the dough out on a lightly floured surface and knead it a few times until it comes together.

6. Using a rolling pin, roll the dough out to a ¼-inch thickness.

7. Slice the dough into a grid to create squares, rectangles, or triangles. Alternatively, use cookie cutters to cut out the desired shapes. Place the bars or shapes on the prepared baking sheet.

8. Bake the treats until the edges are golden brown, 20 to 25 minutes.

9. Remove the treats from the oven and let them cool completely.

10. Store the treats in an airtight container for up to 3 days at room temperature or up to 3 months in the freezer.

**TIP** Substitute dried cranberries instead of fresh for a slightly chewier texture.

Per serving (1 of 15 total): Calories: 131; Protein: 6g; Fat: 2g; Carbs: 26g

# BLUEBERRY BARS

PREP TIME: 15 MINUTES / COOK TIME: 30 MINUTES

*Many people only think of treats as treats, almost like it shows a little extra love. However, the real value of healthy snacks is that they replenish the body with a bit of extra fuel to keep us going. With some carbs, protein, and a pop of blueberry, these bars are always welcome on a trail.* **MAKES 15 TO 30 TREATS**

1 cup steel-cut rolled oats

1 cup fresh blueberries

2 large eggs

3 cups whole-wheat flour, divided, plus more for flouring

1. Preheat the oven to 350°F. Line a baking sheet with parchment paper or a silicone baking mat and set aside.

2. In the bowl of an electric mixer fitted with the paddle attachment, beat the oats, blueberries, and eggs on medium-high speed until well mixed, 1 to 2 minutes.

3. Reduce the speed to low and gradually add 2½ cups flour, beating until just mixed.

4. Beat in the remaining flour, ¼ cup at a time, just until the dough is no longer sticky.

5. Turn the dough out on a lightly floured surface and knead it a few times until it comes together.

6. Using a rolling pin, roll the dough out to a ¼-inch thickness.

7. Slice the dough into a grid to create squares, rectangles, or triangles. Alternatively, use cookie cutters to cut out the desired shapes. Place the bars or shapes on the prepared baking sheet.

8. Bake the treats until the edges are golden brown, 20 to 25 minutes.

9. Remove the treats from the oven and let them cool completely.

10. Store the treats in an airtight container for up to 3 days at room temperature or up to 3 months in the freezer.

**TIP** I also to bake these a little thicker as a sheet and cut them into bars after they cool.

Per serving (1 of 15 total): Calories: 134; Protein: 6g; Fat: 2g; Carbs: 26g

# PEANUT BUTTER AND PUMPKIN COOKIES

PREP TIME: 15 MINUTES / COOK TIME: 30 MINUTES

*I've never been one for treat training; it is all too common that a dog will be able to see the treat and learn the association. This can very easily lead to a dog only doing a "trick" to receive a treat. I personally like to use praise as a reward for good behavior to avoid any confusion. That being said, it can be a fun activity to give your dog cookies once in a while, and there's nothing wrong with that.* **MAKES 15 TO 30 TREATS**

⅔ cup pumpkin purée

¼ cup peanut butter

2 large eggs

3 cups almond flour, divided, plus more for flouring

1. Preheat the oven to 350°F. Line a baking sheet with parchment paper or a silicone baking mat and set aside.

2. In the bowl of an electric mixer fitted with the paddle attachment, beat the pumpkin purée, peanut butter, and eggs on medium-high until well mixed, 1 to 2 minutes

3. Reduce the speed to low and gradually add 2½ cups of flour, beating until just mixed.

4. Beat in the remaining flour, ¼ cup at a time, just until the dough is no longer sticky.

5. Turn the dough out on a lightly floured surface and knead it a few times until it comes together.

6. Using a rolling pin, roll the dough out to a ¼-inch thickness.

CONTINUED

7. Using cookie cutters, cut out the desired shapes and place them on the prepared baking sheet.

8. Bake the cookies until the edges are golden brown, 20 to 25 minutes.

9. Remove the cookies from the oven and let them cool completely.

10. Store the cookies in an airtight container for up to 3 days at room temperature or up to 3 months in the freezer.

**TIP** Keep your treats out of sight when giving a command, like "sit," for example. Once the command is executed, give the reward of verbal praise ("good job, buddy"), then give the dog the treat. When the dog can see the treat, it's not uncommon for them to just run through all the tricks they know, without listening for a command and responding.

Per serving (1 of 15 total): Calories: 166; Protein: 7g; Fat: 14g; Carbs: 7g

# ZUCCHINI TREATZ

PREP TIME: 15 MINUTES / COOK TIME: 30 MINUTES

*These are a healthy little snack, whether you're out and need a quick energy boost or just feel like surprising your pal with a treat. These are a simple, low-calorie snack for any time.* **MAKES 15 TO 30 TREATS**

2 large eggs

3 cups almond flour, plus
  more for flouring

½ cup puréed zucchini

1. Preheat the oven to 350°F. Line a large baking sheet with parchment paper or aluminum foil and set aside.

2. In the bowl of the electric mixer fitted with the paddle attachment, beat the eggs on low speed until blended.

3. Add the almond flour and zucchini and mix until a tacky dough forms. If the dough is too sticky, add more flour, 1 tablespoon at a time (but not more than ½ cup overall).

4. Turn the dough out on a lightly floured surface and knead it a few times until it comes together.

5. Using a rolling pin lightly coated with almond flour, roll out the dough to a ¼-inch thickness.

6. Using cookie cutters, cut out the desired shapes and place them on the prepared baking sheet.

7. Bake the treats until they are dry and the edges are golden, 18 to 20 minutes.

8. For the crispiest treats, transfer them immediately to a wire rack to cool completely.

9. Store the treats in an airtight container for up to 3 days at room temperature or up to 3 months in the freezer.

**TIP** Sometimes, I like to add some of these treats directly into a meal. The treats add a little crunch and another flavor. This addition is not likely to upset your dog's stomach since they are already a familiar snack.

Per serving (1 of 15 total): Calories: 139; Protein: 6g; Fat: 12g; Carbs: 5g

# PEANUT BUTTER AND BANANA COOKIES

PREP TIME: 15 MINUTES / COOK TIME: 30 MINUTES

*Peanut butter, bananas, and blueberries are delicious. These cookies speak for themselves. If your dog is lucky enough that you share these, they will absolutely love them. They are packed with potassium, vitamins, antioxidants, and protein, so they're healthy, too!* **MAKES 15 TO 30 TREATS**

2 bananas

1 cup fresh blueberries

⅔ cup peanut butter

2 large eggs

3 cups almond flour, divided, plus more for flouring

1. Preheat the oven to 350°F. Line a baking sheet with parchment paper or a silicone baking mat and set aside.

2. Purée the bananas and blueberries in a food processor or blender.

3. Transfer the purée to the bowl of an electric mixer fitted with the paddle attachment. Add the peanut butter and eggs and beat on medium-high speed until well mixed, 1 to 2 minutes.

4. Reduce the speed to low and gradually add 2½ cups of flour, beating until just mixed.

5. Beat in the remaining flour, ¼ cup at a time, just until the dough is no longer sticky.

6. Turn the dough out on a lightly floured surface and knead it a few times until it comes together.

7. Using a rolling pin, roll the dough out to a ¼-inch thickness.

8. Using cookie cutters, cut out the desired shapes and place them on the prepared baking sheet.

9. Bake until the edges are golden brown, 20 to 25 minutes.

10. Remove the cookies from the oven and let them cool completely.

11. Store the cookies in an airtight container for up to 3 days at room temperature or up to 3 months in the freezer.

> **TIP** If you've got bananas that are starting to brown, you can peel them, cut them into halves or slices, and pop them in the freezer in sealed freezer bags to preserve them longer.

Per serving (1 of 15 total): Calories: 224; Protein: 9g; Fat: 18g; Carbs: 12g

# BACON BITES

PREP TIME: 15 MINUTES / COOK TIME: 30 MINUTES

*These treats are a bit high in sodium and fat, so use them moderately rather than every day. That being said, there is only a small amount of bacon in here, and the sweet potatoes provide vitamins A, B$_6$, and C, calcium, potassium, and iron.* **MAKES 15 TO 30 TREATS**

| | | |
|---|---|---|
| 1 sweet potato, peeled and cut into 1-inch chunks | 2 bacon slices, cooked<br>2 large eggs | 3 cups almond flour, plus more for flouring |

1. Preheat the oven to 350°F. Line a large baking sheet with parchment paper or aluminum foil and set aside.

2. Place the sweet potato in a medium saucepan over high heat. Add water to cover the sweet potato by 1 inch. Bring to a boil, then reduce the heat to low, cover, and simmer for 30 minutes or until the sweet potato is soft.

3. Drain the sweet potato and transfer it to a food processor. Add the bacon and purée the mixture.

4. Transfer the sweet potato and bacon mixture to the bowl of the electric mixer fitted with the paddle attachment. Add the eggs and beat on medium until blended.

5. Add in the almond flour and beat until a tacky dough forms. If the dough is too sticky, add more flour 1 tablespoon at a time (but not more than ½ cup overall).

6. Turn the dough out on a lightly floured surface and knead it a few times until it comes together.

7. Using a rolling pin lightly coated with flour, roll out the dough to a ¼-inch thickness.

8. Using cookie cutters, cut out the desired shapes and place them on the prepared baking sheet.

9. Bake the treats until they are dry and the edges are golden, about 20 minutes. Using tongs or a spatula, flip the treats and bake for another 10 minutes.

10. Remove the treats from the oven and let them cool completely.

11. Store the treats in an airtight container for up to 3 days at room temperature or up to 3 months in the freezer.

**TIP** A hearty snack can be a fun treat, but always be aware of how many treats you are giving your dog. This one is especially filling and should be accounted for by reducing the food portion of their next meal.

Per serving (1 of 15 total): Calories: 153; Protein: 6g; Fat: 12g; Carbs: 7g

# PUMPKIN COOKIES

PREP TIME: 15 MINUTES / COOK TIME: 30 MINUTES

*This recipe is about as simple as they come—just pumpkin, flour, and eggs. It's a perfect low-calorie treat that doesn't add up quickly in calories, so they shouldn't have much of an impact on feeding time.*

**MAKES 15 TO 30 TREATS**

1 cup pumpkin purée

2 large eggs

3 cups whole-wheat flour, divided, plus more for flouring

1. Preheat the oven to 350°F. Line a baking sheet with parchment paper or a silicone baking mat and set aside.
2. In the bowl of an electric mixer fitted with the paddle attachment, beat the pumpkin and eggs on medium-high speed until well mixed, 1 to 2 minutes.
3. Reduce the speed to low and gradually add 2½ cups of flour, beating just until mixed.
4. Beat in the remaining flour, ¼ cup at a time, just until the dough is no longer sticky.
5. Turn the dough out on a lightly floured surface and knead it a few times until it comes together.
6. Using a rolling pin, roll the dough out to a ¼-inch thickness.
7. Using cookie cutters, cut out the desired shapes and place them on the prepared baking sheet.
8. Bake the cookies until the edges are golden brown, 20 to 25 minutes.
9. Remove the cookies from the oven and let them cool completely.
10. Store the cookies in an airtight container for up to 3 days at room temperature or up to 3 months in the freezer.

**TIP** If you do choose to use treats as a training aid, these are a great choice. Given the low calories and benefits for digestion, these are an ideal choice if you're going to be using a lot of them.

Per serving (1 of 15 total): Calories: 96; Protein: 4g; Fat: 1g; Carbs: 19g

# APPLE, PEANUT BUTTER, AND PUMPKIN BITES

PREP TIME: 15 MINUTES / COOK TIME: 30 MINUTES

*Adding apples and peanut butter to simple pumpkin cookies make these another excellent choice for replenishment on hikes or long walks. Since they have some protein and other vitamins, they will help keep you going if you're running out of steam.*

**MAKES 15 TO 30 TREATS**

2 apples, cored
  and chopped

1 cup pumpkin purée

⅔ cup peanut butter

2 large eggs

2½ to 3 cups whole-wheat
  flour, plus more for flouring

1. Preheat the oven to 350°F. Line a baking sheet with parchment paper or a silicone baking mat and set aside.

2. Place the apples in a blender or food processor and purée.

3. Transfer the apples to the bowl of an electric mixer fitted with the paddle attachment. Add the pumpkin, peanut butter, and eggs and beat on medium-high speed until well mixed, 1 to 2 minutes.

4. Reduce the speed to low and gradually add 2½ cups of flour, beating just until a tacky dough forms. If the dough is too sticky, add more flour, 1 tablespoon at a time (but not more than ½ cup overall).

5. Turn the dough out on a lightly floured surface and knead it a few times until it comes together.

CONTINUED

6. Using a rolling pin, roll the dough out to a ¼-inch thickness.

7. Using cookie cutters, cut out the desired shapes and place them on the prepared baking sheet.

8. Bake the treats until the edges are golden brown, 20 to 25 minutes.

9. Remove the treats from the oven and let them cool completely.

10. Store the treats in an airtight container for up to 3 days at room temperature or up to 3 months in the freezer.

**TIP** Cranberries are great in this one, too! Try substituting fresh cranberries or blueberries for the pumpkin in this recipe.

Per serving (1 of 15 total): Calories: 159; Protein: 7g; Fat: 7g; Carbs: 21g

# BLUCCHINI BITES

*Blueberries are packed with antioxidants, vitamins C and K, as well as fiber, calcium, zinc, manganese, magnesium, and phosphorus. Carrots provide some of the same nutrients, along with beta-carotene. The zucchini is a tasty low-calorie addition.* **MAKES 15 TO 30 TREATS**

¾ cup coarsely
   chopped zucchini

¾ cup coarsely
   chopped carrots

1 cup fresh blueberries

2 large eggs

3½ cups whole-wheat flour,
   plus more for flouring

1. Preheat the oven to 350°F. Line a large baking sheet with parchment paper or aluminum foil and set aside.

2. Place the zucchini and carrots in a food processor and purée.

3. In the bowl of the electric mixer fitted with the paddle attachment, beat the blueberries and eggs together on medium-high speed until blended.

4. Add the flour and zucchini-carrot mixture and beat until a tacky dough forms. If the dough is too sticky, add more flour, 1 tablespoon at a time (but not more than ½ cup overall).

5. Turn the dough out on a lightly floured surface and knead it a few times until it comes together.

6. Using a rolling pin lightly coated with flour, roll out the dough to a ¼-inch thickness.

**CONTINUED**

7. Using cookie cutters, cut out the desired shapes and place them on the prepared baking sheet.

8. Bake the treats until they are dry and the edges are golden, 18 to 20 minutes.

9. For the crispiest treats, transfer them immediately to a wire rack to cool completely.

10. Store the treats in an airtight container for up to 3 days at room temperature or up to 3 months in the freezer.

**TIP** Zucchini should make up less than 10 percent of your dog's daily diet, so if you're planning on feeding zucchini dishes, give one of the other treats while doing so.

Per serving (1 of 15 total): Calories: 114; Protein: 5g; Fat: 1g; Carbs: 23g

# CRAN-ZUCCHINI BITES

PREP TIME: 15 MINUTES / COOK TIME: 30 MINUTES

*With this recipe, you can substitute dried cranberries for a slightly chewier bar. Also, try adding some steel-cut oats into the mix. I always share these with my dogs out on a hike.* **MAKES 15 TO 30 TREATS**

¾ cup coarsely
  chopped zucchini
½ cup baby spinach

½ cup fresh cranberries
2 large eggs

3½ cups whole-wheat flour,
  plus more for flouring

1.  Preheat the oven to 350°F. Line a large baking sheet with parchment paper or aluminum foil and set aside.

2.  Place the zucchini and spinach into a food processor and purée.

3.  In the bowl of the electric mixer fitted with the paddle attachment, beat the cranberries and eggs together on medium-high speed until blended.

4.  Add the flour and zucchini-spinach mixture and beat until just incorporated. If the dough is too sticky, add more flour, 1 tablespoon at a time (but not more than ½ cup overall).

5.  Turn the dough out on a lightly floured surface and knead it a few times until it comes together.

6.  Using a rolling pin lightly coated with flour, roll out the dough to a ¼-inch thickness.

7.  Using cookie cutters, cut out the desired shapes and place them on the prepared baking sheet.

8.  Bake the treats until they are dry and the edges are golden, 18 to 20 minutes.

9.  For the crispiest treats, transfer them immediately to a wire rack to cool completely.

10. Store the treats in an airtight container for up to 3 days at room temperature or up to 3 months in the freezer.

**TIP** Zucchini can be left out of these bites without affecting the texture. If you want to make these but have already given your dog a zucchini meal, just leave it out.

Per serving (1 of 15 total): Calories: 108; Protein: 5g; Fat: 1g; Carbs: 21g

# BLUEBERRY YOGURT CUBES

PREP TIME: 5 MINUTES

*Frozen treats are so good on a hot day! There's no reason the whole family (furry or not) can't enjoy these at a picnic.* **MAKES 4 TO 8 TREATS**

½ cup plain yogurt
½ cup fresh blueberries

1. Place the yogurt and blueberries in a blender or food processor and purée.

2. Spoon the mixture into ice cube trays and freeze overnight.

3. Store leftovers in an airtight container in the freezer for up to 3 months.

**TIP** This recipe is really versatile. I like to use cranberries, pumpkin, bananas, or watermelon to add variety.

Per serving (1 of 4 total): Calories: 29; Protein: 2g; Fat: 1g; Carbs: 5g

# CHICKEN JERKY

PREP TIME: 20 MINUTES / COOK TIME: 2 HOURS

*Dried chicken jerky strips are pure protein. I have yet to meet a dog who didn't love chicken strips, and they are a perfect reward treat to bring on walks. When cooking, the thinner they are sliced, the less time they will take to dehydrate.* **MAKES ABOUT 30–36 STRIPS**

1 pound skinless boneless
  chicken breasts or
  thighs, boiled

1 tablespoon olive oil

1. Preheat the oven to 175°F.

2. Place your boiled chicken on a cutting board, remove any excess fat and discard. Slice the chicken into thin strips about ⅛-inch thick, cutting with the grain.

3. Brush a baking sheet or baking pan with olive oil.

4. Lay out the chicken strips on the oiled baking sheets, leaving space in between; place into oven.

5. Set a timer for 2 hours. If the chicken is not crispy after 2 hours, and there is still moisture remaining, check them every hour until they are fully dehydrated.

6. When the chicken strips are dehydrated, carefully remove them from the oven and transfer them to a cooling rack.

7. Once cool, store in an airtight container. They should last 4 to 6 weeks at room temperature.

**TIP** Using cooked chicken greatly reduces the chance of bacteria remaining on the meat. If dehydrating chicken in the oven, instead of in a dehydrator, it is possible for the moisture to be removed, without the chicken ever actually hitting the 165°F temperature needed to kill off bacteria.

Per serving (30 per recipe): Calories: 19; Protein: 3g; Fat: 1g; Carbs: 0g

# CHICKEN AND RICE SNACKS

*Another healthy cookie for a boost, reward, or treat. Whatever you call it, this is a healthy snack that will taste great!* **MAKES ABOUT 30 TREATS**

½ cup white rice

½ pound boiled skinless
    boneless chicken

2 large eggs

3 cups whole-wheat flour

1. In a medium covered pot, bring the white rice and 1 cup of water to a rapid boil. Reduce to a simmer for 15 minutes, or until all the water is absorbed.

2. Preheat oven to 350°F. Line a large baking sheet with parchment paper, and set aside.

3. Place the boiled chicken into a food processor, and pulse until smooth.

4. In the bowl of an electric mixer, beat the white rice and eggs together until blended.

5. Add in the whole-wheat flour and chicken purée until just incorporated. (If the dough is really sticky, add a little more flour until the dough is tacky but not dry.)

6. Place the dough on a lightly floured surface and knead a few times until it comes together.

7. Using a rolling pin lightly coated with flour, roll out the dough to about a ¼-inch thickness.

8. Using cookie cutters, cut out the desired shapes and transfer to the prepared baking sheet.

9. Place in the oven and bake until the treats are dry and edges are golden, about 20 minutes.

10. Carefully remove from the oven, and transfer onto a cooling rack.

11. Once cool, store in an airtight container. They should last 4 weeks in the refrigerator.

**TIP** Change out the white rice in this recipe for brown rice for an even healthier snack.

Per serving (30 per recipe): Calories: 64; Protein: 4g; Fat: 1g; Carbs: 11g

# CHICKEN AND SWEET POTATO TREATS

PREP TIME: 60 MINUTES / COOK TIME: 90 MINUTES

*Chicken and sweet potato treats are a tasty way to keep your dog satiated. With protein and carbs, these treats will help fuel long hikes. They taste great and they're easy to carry.* **MAKES ABOUT 30 TREATS**

½ pound boiled boneless skinless chicken

2 medium sweet potatoes, halved lengthwise

2 large eggs
3 cups whole-wheat flour

1. Preheat the oven to 400°F.

2. Place the sweet potatoes on a baking pan or baking sheet. (For easier cleanup, line the sheet with parchment paper.)

3. Put the sweet potatoes in the oven and set a timer for 25 to 35 minutes, depending on the size of your halves.

4. When the potatoes are done, carefully remove them, and turn the oven down to 350°F.

5. Once the potatoes are cooled, scoop the potatoes out of their skins and into a food processor. Add the boiled chicken, and chop.

6. In the bowl of the electric mixer, beat the eggs with the chicken and sweet potato mixture until blended.

7. Add in the whole-wheat flour until just incorporated. (If the dough is really sticky, you'll need to add a little more flour, just a little bit at a time though, and not more than ½ cup overall. You want the dough to be just a little tacky.)

8. Place the dough on a surface lightly sprinkled with flour and knead a few times until it comes together.

9. Using a rolling pin lightly coated with whole-wheat flour, roll out the dough to about a ¼-inch thickness.

**CONTINUED**

10. Using cookie cutters, cut out the desired shapes and transfer to the prepared baking sheet.

11. Place in the oven and bake until the treats are dry and edges are golden, about 20 minutes.

12. Carefully remove from the oven, and transfer onto a cooling rack.

13. Once cool, store in an airtight container. They should last 4 weeks in the refrigerator.

**TIP** Plain sweet potato fries also make great treats. Peel and cut potatoes into fry shapes, and bake at 375°F for 20 minutes.

Per serving (30 per recipe): Calories: 62; Protein: 4g; Fat: 1g; Carbs: 11g

# FROZEN BANANA AND HONEY CUBES

PREP TIME: 10 MINUTES / COOK TIME: AROUND 4 HOURS

*With banana, honey, Greek yogurt, and pumpkin, these refreshing treats taste great, and are beneficial all the way through to digestion. Using locally farmed honey is another great way to help fight off allergies.* **MAKES ABOUT 20 CUBES**

½ cup plain Greek yogurt

½ cup pumpkin purée

½ cup honey

½ cup banana

1. Place your banana, pumpkin purée, honey, and yogurt in a food processor, and purée.

2. Fill ice cube trays with the purée, and freeze overnight.

3. These treats will keep in an airtight container in the freezer for up to 3 months.

**TIP** Locally sourced honey is a fantastic way to combat allergies because there are small amounts of pollen from all the local plants in the honey.

Per serving (20 per recipe): Calories: 37; Protein: 1g; Fat: <1g; Carbs: 9g

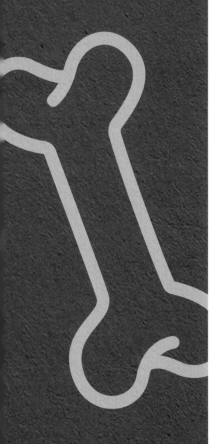

## MEATY MAINS

### Chapter Five

Here is the heart of your dog's daily diet—hearty entreés that are packed with protein and an array of the vitamins and minerals needed for a well-balanced diet. When introducing new cooked foods to your pet, take the time to note any changes in behaviors and watch for any symptoms of allergic reactions.

# TUNA NOODLE

PREP TIME: 10 MINUTES / COOK TIME: 25 MINUTES

*Tuna is a great source of protein and fatty acids, including omega-3s and omega-6s. These nutrients support healthy brain function, a shiny coat, and healthy joints. Your dogs will love this meal and with a little extra seasoning. I think you'll enjoy it, too!* **MAKES 10 CUPS**

| | | |
|---|---|---|
| 10 cups water, divided | 2 cups chopped zucchini | 1 (5-ounce) can |
| 8 ounces dried macaroni | 2 cups peas | water-packed tuna |

1. Bring 8 cups of water to a boil in a large stockpot over medium-high heat. Add the macaroni and cook until al dente, about 8 minutes.

2. While the macaroni is cooking, bring the remaining 2 cups of water to a boil in a medium saucepan fitted with a steamer basket over high heat. Add the zucchini and peas and steam for 15 minutes, or until tender.

3. Drain the macaroni and transfer it to a large bowl. Stir in the steamed zucchini and peas and the tuna with its liquid.

4. Let cool. Serve as is or purée in a food processor, depending on your dog's size.

5. Store leftovers in an airtight container or portioned into sealed plastic bags in the refrigerator for up to 1 week or in the freezer for 3 months.

**TIP** If your dog is not used to a fish diet, introduce fish slowly to make sure they don't have an allergic reaction or gastrointestinal discomfort. The same caution should be used when giving anything to your dog that they have never had before.

Per 1 cup serving: Calories: 118; Protein: 7g; Fat: 1g; Carbs: 22g

# SALMON AND RICE

PREP TIME: 20 MINUTES / COOK TIME: 45 MINUTES

*Salmon is a fantastic source of protein. This fish is rich with omega-3 and omega-6 fatty acids, which are crucial nutrients for promoting joint health. Joints can be a concern for all breeds, mixes, and sizes of dogs. If you include fatty acids regularly in their diet, as your dog gets older, they'll be ahead of the game and you won't have to spend a fortune on supplements.* **MAKES 10 CUPS**

4 cups water

2 cups brown rice

8 ounces boneless
salmon fillet

2 cups chopped cucumber

1 cup chopped apples

1. Place the water and rice in a large saucepan over medium-high heat and bring to a boil. Reduce the heat to low, cover, and simmer until the rice is tender and the liquid absorbed, about 45 minutes.

2. Meanwhile, preheat the oven to 400°F.

3. Place a 12-inch piece of aluminum foil on a work surface and place the salmon fillet in the center. Cover the fish with the cucumber and apples, and fold the edges of the foil up to form a sealed packet.

4. When the rice has 15 minutes left, place the packet in a small baking dish and bake until the salmon is cooked through, 10 to 15 minutes.

5. Remove the packet from the oven and carefully transfer the contents into the rice. With a fork, mix it all together, breaking up or flaking the salmon as you go.

6. Let the mixture cool before serving.

7. Store leftovers in an airtight container or portioned into sealed plastic bags in the refrigerator for up to 1 week or in the freezer for 3 months.

**TIP** Fish bones are a real concern, so it is important to ensure they are all removed. Place a bowl upside down on the counter and lay the fish on its back arched over the bowl. Then run your hands over the fish, and if you feel any bones, remove them.

Per 1 cup serving: Calories: 164; Protein: 8g; Fat: 2g; Carbs: 30g

# TUNA, RICE, AND PEAS

PREP TIME: 5 MINUTES / COOK TIME: 20 MINUTES

*Over the years, I have seen a lot of different diets, beliefs, routines, and cuisines related to dogs, and one thing they all have in common are fish blends. It's easy to see the benefits of fish, and it's not something that should be overlooked.* **MAKES 10 CUPS**

6 cups water, divided
2 cups white rice

8 ounces frozen peas
and carrots

1 (5-ounce) can
water-packed tuna

1. Place 4 cups of water and the rice in a large saucepan over medium-high heat and bring to a boil. Reduce the heat to low, cover, and simmer until the rice is tender and the liquid is absorbed, about 20 minutes.

2. Meanwhile, bring the remaining 2 cups of water to a boil in a medium saucepan fitted with a steamer basket. Add the peas and carrots, cover, and steam for about 10 minutes, or until tender.

3. Using a food processor, purée the cooked peas and carrots and set aside.

4. Transfer the rice to a large bowl, add the puréed vegetables and tuna with its liquid, and mix together well.

5. Let the mixture cool before serving.

6. Store leftovers in an airtight container or portioned into sealed plastic bags in the refrigerator for up to 1 week or in the freezer for 3 months.

**TIP** Tuna is high in mercury, so it should be consumed by dogs in moderation.

Per 1 cup serving: Calories: 159; Protein: 6g; Fat: 1g; Carbs: 33g

# SHRIMP AND QUINOA

PREP TIME: 5 MINUTES / COOK TIME: 30 MINUTES

*Shrimp is a great source of protein and is easy to prepare. This tender shellfish can be high in cholesterol, so while this recipe has other health benefits, it should reserved as a special meal. The American Kennel Club (AKC) promotes shrimp for its phosphorus, which is necessary for your dog's bone health, and plentiful antioxidants, which can help fight disease.* **MAKES 6 CUPS**

4 cups water, divided
1 cup quinoa, rinsed
1 cup chopped green beans
  (about 2-inch pieces)

1 tablespoon unsalted
  butter or olive oil

8 ounces frozen peeled and
  deveined shrimp, thawed
  and tails removed

1. Place 2 cups of water and the quinoa in a large saucepan over medium-high heat and bring to a boil. Reduce the heat to low, cover, and simmer until the quinoa is tender, about 15 minutes. Remove the saucepan from the heat and let stand 5 minutes. Transfer to a large bowl.

2. Meanwhile, bring the remaining 2 cups of water to a boil in a medium saucepan fitted with a steamer basket. Add the green beans, cover, and steam for about 10 minutes, or until tender. Add the green beans to the bowl of quinoa.

3. Melt the butter in a small skillet over medium-high heat. Add the shrimp and sauté until cooked through, about 5 minutes.

4. Chop the shrimp, add it to the quinoa mixture, and stir to combine.

5. Let the mixture cool before serving.

6. Store leftovers in an airtight container or portioned into sealed plastic bags in the refrigerator for up to 1 week or in the freezer for 3 months.

**TIP** Using store-bought precooked shrimp will eliminate step 3. It won't cut the cooking time down by much, but it will be one less thing to worry about, and the dogs will still love it!

Per 1 cup serving: Calories: 164; Protein: 10g; Fat: 4g; Carbs: 22g

# SWEET POTATO COD

PREP TIME: 10 MINUTES / COOK TIME: 50 MINUTES

*Cod is a healthy protein. It's rich in omega-3 and omega-6 fatty acids, and it's delicious. To check if your fish is cooked through, poke it with a fork and twist. If the fish flakes easily and is opaque, it is done.*

**MAKES 6 CUPS**

2 to 3 sweet potatoes, scrubbed and halved lengthwise

3 tablespoons unsalted butter, divided

8 ounces cod

1 cup baby spinach

1 chopped green beans (about 2-inch pieces)

1. Preheat the oven to 400°F. Line a baking sheet with parchment paper or aluminum foil.

2. Place the sweet potatoes, cut-side up, on the prepared baking sheet. Bake until tender, 25 to 35 minutes.

3. Meanwhile, melt 2 tablespoons of butter in a medium skillet over medium-high heat. Add the cod and cook for 2 minutes on one side. Reduce the heat to medium-low, flip the cod over, add the remaining 1 tablespoon of butter, and let it melt.

4. Add the spinach and green beans and cook, stirring occasionally, until the vegetables are tender and the cod is flaky and opaque, 10 to 15 minutes.

5. Chop the sweet potatoes and transfer them to a large bowl. Add the vegetables and cod and mix everything together.

6. Let cool before serving.

7. Store leftovers in an airtight container or portioned into sealed plastic bags in the refrigerator for up to 1 week or in the freezer for 3 months.

**TIP** You can also microwave the sweet potatoes to cut the cooking time. Wash the sweet potato, stab it four times with a fork (on a cutting board, not in your hand, please), wrap it in a paper towel, and place it on a microwave-safe plate. Microwave the potato until tender, about 5 minutes.

Per 1 cup serving: Calories: 143; Protein: 10g; Fat: 6g; Carbs: 12g

# TURKEY MAC 'N' CRANBERRIES

PREP TIME: 10 MINUTES / COOK TIME: 45 MINUTES

*Turkey recipes are a favorite of mine. I tend to like lean ground turkey for many of my family recipes, so I often buy in bulk without worrying it will go bad. I also tend to make many different turkey-based recipes since my dogs happen to thrive with turkey as their main source of protein. It is an advantage to feed the dogs a variety of turkey recipes because it is unlikely they will develop an allergy to this ingredient.*

**MAKES 6 CUPS**

| | | |
|---|---|---|
| 2 sweet potatoes, scrubbed and halved lengthwise | 8 ounces dried macaroni | 1 cup fresh cranberries |
| | 1 pound ground turkey | |

1. Preheat the oven to 400°F. Line a baking sheet with parchment paper or aluminum foil.

2. Place the sweet potatoes, cut-side up, on the prepared baking sheet. Bake until tender, 25 to 35 minutes.

3. Meanwhile, bring a large pot of water to boil over high heat. Add the macaroni and cook until al dente, about 8 minutes.

4. While the pasta cooks, heat a large skillet over medium-high heat. Add the turkey and sauté until it is cooked through and browned, about 10 minutes.

5. Remove the turkey from the heat and drain the excess fat from the skillet. Add the drained pasta and cranberries to the turkey.

6. Chop the baked sweet potatoes and add them to the skillet, stirring to combine.

7. Let the mixture cool before serving.

8. Store leftovers in an airtight container or portioned into sealed plastic bags in the refrigerator for up to 1 week or in the freezer for 3 months.

**TIP** When you cook lean turkey, the leftover bits in the skillet and oil are perfect for a nice gravy. Just add a couple of teaspoons of flour and a cup of broth and stir over medium heat until thickened and creamy.

Per 1 cup serving: Calories: 293; Protein: 20g; Fat: 6g; Carbs: 41g

# TURKEY AND GREEN BEANS

PREP TIME: 5 MINUTES / COOK TIME: 30 MINUTES

*Green beans are a great source of protein, fiber, minerals like iron and calcium, and vitamins like B$_6$, A, C, and K. Green beans are available in cans and frozen, so go ahead and buy them in bulk.* **MAKES 10 CUPS**

6 cups water, divided
2 cups white rice

1 cup chopped green beans
(about 2-inch pieces)
1 cup chopped carrots

1 pound ground turkey
2 large eggs

1. Place 4 cups of water and the rice in a large saucepan over medium-high heat and bring to a boil. Reduce the heat to low, cover, and simmer until the rice is tender and the liquid is absorbed, about 20 minutes.

2. Meanwhile, bring the remaining 2 cups of water to a boil in a medium saucepan fitted with a steamer basket. Add the green beans and carrots, cover, and steam for about 10 minutes, or until tender.

3. Heat a large skillet over medium-high heat. Add the turkey and sauté until it is cooked through and browned, about 10 minutes.

4. Remove the turkey from the heat and drain the excess fat from the skillet. Set aside.

5. Transfer the steamed vegetables to a food processor and purée.

6. Add the eggs to the rice. Let the eggs cook in the hot rice, mixing them around to ensure they are completely cooked.

7. Add the vegetables and the turkey to the rice, stirring to combine.

8. Let the mixture cool before serving.

9. Store leftovers in an airtight container or portioned into sealed plastic bags in the refrigerator for up to 1 week or in the freezer for 3 months.

**TIP** Puréeing the veggies is an optional step in all of these recipes. It helps ensure there aren't any choking hazards and that none of the veggies get left behind by picky eaters.

Per 1 cup serving: Calories: 222; Protein: 13g; Fat: 4g; Carbs: 32g

# TURKEY AND ZUCCHINI

PREP TIME: 10 MINUTES / COOK TIME: 20 MINUTES

*Cauliflower is a good source of fiber and contains vitamins K and C, calcium, potassium, and folate. This combination of nutrients can help support healthy vision, blood, the liver, muscles, and immune system, as well as boost colon health.* **MAKES 10 CUPS**

| | | |
|---|---|---|
| 4 cups water | 1 pound ground turkey | 1 cup chopped cauliflower |
| 2 cups white rice | 2 cups chopped zucchini | 1 large egg |

1.  Place the water and rice in a large saucepan over medium-high heat and bring to a boil. Reduce the heat to low, cover, and simmer until the rice is tender and the liquid is absorbed, about 20 minutes.

2.  Meanwhile, heat a large skillet over medium-high heat. Add the turkey and sauté until it is cooked through and browned, about 10 minutes.

3.  Reduce the heat to medium and stir in the zucchini and cauliflower. Cook, stirring occasionally, for 6 to 7 minutes, until the vegetables are tender and browned.

4.  Remove the skillet from the heat and crack in the egg. Let the egg cook in the hot food, mixing it around to ensure it is completely cooked.

5.  Add the rice to the skillet and stir to combine.

6.  Cool the mixture and serve.

7.  Store leftovers in an airtight container or portioned into sealed plastic bags in the refrigerator for up to 1 week or in the freezer for 3 months.

**TIP** A small sprinkle of fresh or dried parsley will help settle your dog's stomach, if needed, and this herb will also help freshen breath. You can sprinkle a little parsley into most recipes as a healthy breath freshener.

Per 1 cup serving: Calories: 215; Protein: 13g; Fat: 4g; Carbs: 32g

# TURKEY WITH PEAS AND PUMPKIN

PREP TIME: 5 MINUTES / COOK TIME: 45 MINUTES

*Pumpkin is a healthy ingredient and dogs generally love the sweet flavor, so I add it to a lot of meals and treats for my dogs. It's a great source of fiber and good for their digestive system. Keeping things moving smoothly through the digestive system is always important for your dog.* **MAKES 10 CUPS**

6 cups water, divided

2 cups brown rice

1 pound ground turkey

2 cups peas

2 large eggs

2 tablespoons pumpkin purée

1. Place 4 cups of water and the rice in a large saucepan over medium-high heat and bring to a boil. Reduce the heat to low, cover, and simmer until the rice is tender and the liquid is absorbed, about 45 minutes.

2. Meanwhile, heat a large skillet over medium-high heat. Add the turkey and sauté until it is cooked through and browned, about 10 minutes.

3. Remove the turkey from the heat and drain the excess fat from the skillet. Set aside.

4. Bring the remaining 2 cups of water to a boil in a medium saucepan fitted with a steamer basket. Add the peas, cover, and steam for about 10 minutes, or until tender.

5. Remove the lid from the cooked rice and crack the eggs on top. Let stand for 1 minute so the eggs can cook a little, then stir to mix in and finish cooking the eggs.

6. Add the steamed peas, rice mixture, and pumpkin purée to the turkey, stirring to combine.

7. Let cool before serving.

8. Store leftovers in an airtight container or portioned into sealed plastic bags in the refrigerator for up to 1 week or in the freezer for 3 months.

**TIP** Pumpkin purée can be a little difficult to come by after the holidays, so it pays off to think ahead and stock up when pumpkin pie season comes around.

Per 1 cup serving: Calories: 231; Protein: 15g; Fat: 6g; Carbs: 33g

# SWEET POTATOES AND CHICKEN

PREP TIME: 15 MINUTES / COOK TIME: 60 MINUTES

*Pulled chicken is one of my favorites. I suggest doubling up on the chicken in this recipe and seasoning up the second half for yourself. Try your favorite seasonings or sauces and add the chicken mixture to your dinner menu.* **MAKES 6 CUPS**

2 to 3 sweet potatoes, scrubbed and halved lengthwise

1 pound frozen skinless boneless chicken breasts

2 cups water

1 cup chopped green beans (about 2-inch pieces)

1 apple, chopped

1. Preheat the oven to 400°F. Line a baking sheet with parchment paper or aluminum foil.

2. Place the sweet potatoes, cut-side up, on the baking sheet. Bake until tender, 25 to 35 minutes.

3. Meanwhile, fill a large stockpot over high heat about two-thirds full of water and bring to a boil. Add the chicken, reduce the heat to medium, and simmer until the chicken is cooked through, 15 to 25 minutes.

4. Bring the water to a boil in a medium saucepan fitted with a steamer basket. Add the green beans, cover, and steam for about 10 minutes, or until tender.

5. Remove the cooked chicken from the pot, chop or slice it (depending on your dog's size), and transfer it to a large bowl. Chop the cooked sweet potato and add it to the bowl. Add the steamed green beans and apple, stirring to combine.

6. Let the mixture cool before serving.

7. Store leftovers in an airtight container or portioned into sealed plastic bags in the refrigerator for up to 1 week or in the freezer for 3 months.

**TIP** I always have a bag of frozen skinless boneless chicken breasts in my freezer. This bounty of poultry is handy because it can go directly from the freezer to the stove.

Per 1 cup serving: Calories: 137; Protein: 16g; Fat: 2g; Carbs: 15g

# BLUEBERRY CHICKEN

PREP TIME: 10 MINUTES / COOK TIME: 35 MINUTES

*Blueberries might seem like a strange addition to a chicken dinner, but when you think about it, how different are blueberries and chicken from the combination of cranberries and turkey in a Thanksgiving dinner? Blueberries and chicken are a cleaner version of that dish.*

**MAKES 6 CUPS**

4 cups water, divided

1 cup quinoa, rinsed

1 pound skinless boneless
  chicken breast

1 cup chicken broth

1 cup chopped cauliflower

1 cup fresh blueberries

1. Place 2 cups of water and the quinoa in a medium saucepan over medium-high heat and bring to a boil. Reduce the heat to low and simmer until the quinoa is tender, about 15 minutes. Remove the saucepan from the heat and let stand 5 minutes.

2. Meanwhile, heat a large skillet over medium-high heat. Add the chicken and cook for 5 minutes. Add the chicken broth, cover, and simmer until the chicken is cooked through, about 10 minutes.

3. Bring the remaining 2 cups of water to a boil in a medium saucepan fitted with a steamer basket. Add the cauliflower, cover, and steam for about 10 minutes, or until tender.

4. Transfer the cooked chicken to a large bowl and use two forks to shred the meat. Add the cooked quinoa, cauliflower, and blueberries, stirring to combine.

5. Let the mixture cool before serving.

6. Store leftovers in an airtight container or portioned into sealed plastic bags in the refrigerator for up to 1 week or in the freezer for 3 months.

**TIP** This is such a delicious meal that I suggest you make extra for yourself!

Per 1 cup serving: Calories: 207; Protein: 20g; Fat: 4g; Carbs: 25g

# CHICKEN AND BROCCOLI

PREP TIME: 10 MINUTES / COOK TIME: 35 MINUTES

*I could live on chicken and broccoli. This is such a clean, nutritious meal, and I can almost feel the nutrients in the ingredients making me stronger and healthier. I hope that that is exactly how the dogs feel.*

**MAKES 10 CUPS**

| | | |
|---|---|---|
| 6 cups water, divided | 1 cup broccoli | 2 tablespoons |
| 2 cups white rice | 1 pound ground chicken | pumpkin purée |

1. Place 4 cups of water and the rice in a large saucepan over medium-high heat and bring to a boil. Reduce the heat to low, cover, and simmer until the rice is tender and the liquid is absorbed, about 20 minutes.

2. Meanwhile, bring the remaining 2 cups of water to a boil in a medium saucepan fitted with a steamer basket. Add the broccoli, cover, and for about 10 minutes, or until tender.

3. Heat a large skillet over medium-high heat. Add the chicken and sauté until it is cooked through and browned, about 10 minutes.

4. Remove the chicken from the heat and drain the excess fat from the skillet. Set aside.

5. Transfer the steamed broccoli to a food processor and purée.

6. Add the cooked rice, broccoli, and pumpkin purée to the chicken, stirring to combine.

7. Let cool before serving.

8. Store leftovers in an airtight container or portioned into sealed plastic bags in the refrigerator for up to 1 week or in the freezer for 3 months.

**TIP** The AKC states that broccoli and cauliflower in excesses can cause gastric irritation in some dogs, so it's always good to space out feeding those ingredients to your pet. The AKC also recommends that broccoli be less than 10 percent of your dog's daily intake. Include this ingredient in moderation to take advantage of its fiber and vitamin C.

Per 1 cup serving: Calories: 219; Protein: 11g; Fat: 5g; Carbs: 31g

# CHICKEN WITH BROWN RICE AND ZUCCHINI

PREP TIME: 15 MINUTES / COOK TIME: 45 MINUTES

*Brown rice and zucchini complement each other so nicely. You get a little bit of savory and a little bit of sweet, as well as a heap of nutrients—such a great choice for your beloved dog. When you add chicken and spinach to the combination, you've got a truly tasty dish.*

**MAKES 10 CUPS**

4 cups water

2 cups brown rice

1 pound frozen skinless boneless chicken

2 tablespoons olive oil

1 cup chopped zucchini

2 cups baby spinach

1. Place the water and rice in a large saucepan over medium-high heat and bring to a boil. Reduce the heat to low, cover, and simmer until the rice is tender and the liquid is absorbed, about 45 minutes.

2. Meanwhile, fill a large stockpot over high heat about two-thirds full of water and bring to a boil. Add the chicken, then reduce the heat to medium and simmer until the chicken is cooked through, 15 to 25 minutes.

3. Heat the olive oil in a large skillet over medium-high heat. Add the zucchini and spinach and sauté until they are tender, 6 to 8 minutes. Remove the skillet from the heat.

4. Cut the cooked chicken into bite-size pieces. Add the chicken and cooked rice to the vegetables, stirring to combine.

5. Let cool before serving.

6. Store leftovers in an airtight container or portioned into sealed plastic bags in the refrigerator for up to 1 week or in the freezer for 3 months.

**TIP** To reheat this meal for lunch for yourself, throw it in a large skillet or a wok over medium heat until warmed through, about 10 minutes. Mix a scrambled egg into the dish and cook it through before enjoying your lunch.

Per 1 cup serving: Calories: 201; Protein: 13g; Fat: 5g; Carbs: 29g

# CHICKEN AND LENTILS

PREP TIME: 15 MINUTES / COOK TIME: 45 MINUTES

*I absolutely love boiled chicken recipes because they are an easy backup plan when you are in a time crunch. The fact that you can take the chicken straight from the freezer to the stove means that if you forget to thaw something else for a meal, you've still got options. This is a tasty high-protein meal packed with a punch of vitamins and minerals.* **MAKES 6 CUPS**

1 pound skinless boneless
  chicken breast
4 cups water, divided

1 cup lentils
1 cup chopped green beans
  (about 2-inch pieces)

1 cup chopped carrots

1. Fill a large stockpot over high heat about two-thirds full of water and bring to a boil. Add the chicken, then reduce the heat to medium and simmer until the chicken is cooked through, 15 to 25 minutes.

2. Place 2 cups of water and the lentils in a medium saucepan and bring to a boil. Reduce the heat to low, cover, and simmer until the lentils are tender, about 20 minutes.

3. Meanwhile, bring the remaining 2 cups of water to a boil in a medium saucepan fitted with a steamer basket. Add the green beans and carrots, cover, and steam for about 10 minutes, or until tender.

4. Cut the cooked chicken into bite-size pieces. Transfer to a large bowl.

5. Add the cooked lentils and steamed vegetables, stirring to combine.

6. Let cool before serving.

7. Store leftovers in an airtight container or portioned into sealed plastic bags in the refrigerator for up to 1 week or in the freezer for 3 months.

> **TIP** Lentils are a fantastic source of protein, but they are not enough to be the starring role. They're best in a supporting role, once in a while. You know, kind of like Matt Damon.

Per 1 cup serving: Calories: 188; Protein: 24g; Fat: 2g; Carbs: 20g

# CRANBERRY BEEF

PREP TIME: 5 MINUTES / COOK TIME: 35 MINUTES

*This is a healthy and quick meal and tastes great with any protein you have on hand. For an extra special treat, you can whip up a little gravy for Thanksgiving or Sunday supper. Swap the beef for some shredded chicken to enhance the holiday feel even more!* **MAKES 10 CUPS**

| | | |
|---|---|---|
| 6 cups water, divided | 1 cup chopped carrots | 1 pound ground beef |
| 2 cups white rice | 1 cup baby spinach | 1 cup fresh cranberries |

1. Place 4 cups of water and the rice in a large saucepan over medium-high heat and bring to a boil. Reduce the heat to low, cover, and simmer until the rice is tender and the water is absorbed, about 20 minutes.

2. Meanwhile, bring the remaining 2 cups of water to a boil in a medium saucepan fitted with a steamer basket. Add the carrots and spinach, cover, and steam for about 10 minutes, or until tender.

3. Heat a large skillet over medium-high heat. Add the beef and sauté until it is cooked through and browned, about 10 minutes.

4. Remove the beef from the heat and drain the excess fat from the skillet. Set aside.

5. Transfer the steamed vegetables to a food processor and purée.

6. Add the vegetables, cooked rice, and cranberries to the beef, stirring to combine.

7. Let cool before serving.

8. Store leftovers in an airtight container or portioned into sealed plastic bags in the refrigerator for up to 1 week or in the freezer for 3 months.

**TIP** Always be careful draining the grease from your meat. It is incredibly hot and can splash all over. Also, you don't want to lose all your meat into the sink.

Per 1 cup serving: Calories: 266; Protein: 11g; Fat: 10g; Carbs: 32g

# BEEF, BEANS, AND BANANAS

PREP TIME: 5 MINUTES / COOK TIME: 45 MINUTES

*This recipe sounds a little like a "botched Thanksgiving traditional English tart," but it's a real favorite with the dogs. The bananas add some fiber and potassium, and the cucumber gives the dish a fresh crisp texture. The recipe packs a punch of nutrition and is quick and easy to prepare, especially if you use leftover cooked rice.*

**MAKES 10 CUPS**

| | | |
|---|---|---|
| 6 cups water, divided | 1 cup chopped green beans | 1 cucumber, cut into a |
| 2 cups brown rice | (about 2-inch pieces) | ½-inch dice |
| | 1 pound ground beef | 1 banana, cut into rounds |

1. Place 4 cups of water and the rice in a large saucepan over medium-high heat and bring to a boil. Reduce the heat to low, cover, and simmer until the rice is tender and the water is absorbed, about 45 minutes.

2. Meanwhile, bring the remaining 2 cups of water to a boil in a medium saucepan fitted with a steamer basket. Add the green beans, cover, and steam for about 15 minutes, or until tender.

3. Heat a large skillet over medium-high heat. Add the beef and sauté until it is cooked through and browned, about 10 minutes.

4. Remove the beef from the heat and drain the excess fat from the skillet.

5. Add the cooked rice, green beans, cucumber, and banana to the beef, stirring to combine.

6. Let cool before serving.

7. Store leftovers in an airtight container or portioned into sealed plastic bags in the refrigerator for up to 1 week or in the freezer for 3 months.

**TIP** A box grater is always a good tool to have in the kitchen. If a recipe calls for chopped or diced vegetables, you can mix it up by shredding them instead.

Per 1 cup serving: Calories: 266; Protein: 12g; Fat: 11g; Carbs: 32g

# GROUND BEEF AND MACARONI

PREP TIME: 5 MINUTES / COOK TIME: 20 MINUTES

*This is a great meal for your dogs. It is hearty, filling, quick, and easy. You might find yourself making it time and time again. Switch up the protein with chicken or turkey for variation or substitute the peas for green beans. Any way you make this dish, it's still going to be simple and great.* **MAKES 6 CUPS**

| 8 ounces dried macaroni | 1 zucchini, chopped | 1 pound ground beef |
| 2 cups water | 1 cup peas | |

1. Bring a large pot of water to a boil over high heat. Add the macaroni and cook until al dente, about 8 minutes. Drain the pasta and set aside.

2. Meanwhile, bring the water to a boil in a medium saucepan fitted with a steamer basket. Add the zucchini and peas, cover, and steam for about 10 minutes, or until tender.

3. Heat a large skillet over medium-high heat. Add the beef and sauté until it is cooked through and browned, about 10 minutes.

4. Remove the beef from the heat and drain the excess fat from the skillet.

5. Add the cooked pasta and vegetables to the beef, stirring to combine.

6. Let cool before serving.

7. Store leftovers in an airtight container or portioned into sealed plastic bags in the refrigerator for up to 1 week or in the freezer for 3 months.

**TIP** If you are in a hurry and only have frozen ground beef, you can thaw it in the microwave. Take the beef out of the packaging and place it on a microwave-safe plate. Microwave the beef at 50 percent power for 3 minutes per 1 pound of beef. Flip the beef every 45 seconds or so, making sure no spots are browning and cooking.

Per 1 cup serving: Calories: 358; Protein: 20g; Fat: 17g; Carbs: 33g

# BEEF WITH PUMPKIN

PREP TIME: 10 MINUTES / COOK TIME: 50 MINUTES

*This is a well-rounded recipe, but if you're looking for something with a little extra protein, crack an egg over the brown rice when it is done cooking. Crack the egg onto the hot rice and when it looks like it is sunny-side up, stir it in and remove the rice from the heat. The egg will continue to cook from the heat of the rice and the pot.* **MAKES 10 CUPS**

6 cups water, divided

2 cups brown rice

1 cup peas

1 cup chopped carrots

1 pound ground beef

2 tablespoons pumpkin purée

1. Place 4 cups of water and the rice in a large saucepan over medium-high heat and bring to a boil. Reduce the heat to low, cover, and simmer until the rice is tender and the water is absorbed, about 45 minutes.

2. Meanwhile, bring the remaining 2 cups of water to a boil in a medium saucepan fitted with a steamer basket. Add the peas and carrots, cover, and steam for about 10 minutes, or until tender.

3. Heat a large skillet over medium-high heat. Add the beef and sauté until it is cooked through and browned, about 10 minutes.

4. Remove the beef from the heat and drain the excess fat from the skillet.

5. Add the cooked rice, vegetables, and pumpkin to the beef, stirring to combine.

6. Let cool before serving.

7. Store leftovers in an airtight container or portioned into sealed plastic bags in the refrigerator for up to 1 week or in the freezer for 3 months.

**TIP** This is another quick, easy-to-make recipe, which makes it great for last-minute dinners when you don't have a ton of time.

Per 1 cup serving: Calories: 266; Protein: 12g; Fat: 11g; Carbs: 32g

# BEEF WITH APPLES

PREP TIME: 15 MINUTES / COOK TIME: 25 MINUTES

*This is a tasty recipe, packed full of protein, vitamins, and minerals. The apples and spinach add a wonderful sweet and savory flavor, and the lentils absorb all the flavors!* **MAKES 6 CUPS**

| | | |
|---|---|---|
| 2 cups water | 1 pound ground beef | 2 cups baby spinach |
| 1 cup lentils | 2 tablespoons olive oil | 1 apple, chopped |

1. Place the water and lentils in a large saucepan over medium-high heat and bring to a boil. Reduce the heat to low, cover, and simmer until the lentils are tender, about 20 minutes.

2. Meanwhile, heat a large skillet over medium-high heat. Add the beef and sauté until it is cooked through and browned, about 10 minutes.

3. Remove the beef from the heat and drain the excess fat from the skillet. Set aside.

4. Heat the olive oil in a large skillet over medium-high heat. Add the spinach and apple and sauté until tender, 2 to 3 minutes. Remove the skillet from the heat.

5. Add the cooked lentils and beef into the spinach and apples, stirring to combine.

6. Let cool before serving.

7. Store leftovers in an airtight container or portioned into sealed plastic bags in the refrigerator for up to 1 week or in the freezer for 3 months.

**TIP** When you are draining your meat, stop just a little bit short to save yourself some good fatty oil to use for gravy (see page 104). This is a perfect dish for a thick gravy topping.

Per 1 cup serving: Calories: 355; Protein: 22g; Fat: 21g; Carbs: 20g

## SUMPTUOUS EXTRAS

### Chapter Six

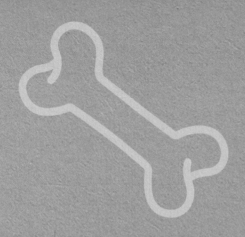

This chapter helps you understand and fulfill a balanced nutritious meal plan for your dog. From proteins to vitamins, these sides are healthy, easy additions for any meal you are serving. These extras can be added to homemade dishes or store-bought food to create a balanced meal, rather than acting as full meals themselves. Some of the ingredients listed—such as broccoli and zucchini—should not make up more than 10 percent of your dog's daily diet. So, make sure you are using these accordingly to suit your dog's needs.

# LENTILS

*Lentils are a great source of protein, and they cook just like white rice. They're a super quick, wonderfully healthy addition to anything.*

**MAKES 2 CUPS**

2 cups water
1 cup lentils

1. Place the water and lentils in a medium saucepan and bring to a boil. Reduce heat to low, cover, and simmer until the lentils are tender, about 20 minutes.

2. Remove the saucepan from the heat.

3. Let cool before serving.

4. Store leftovers in an airtight container in the refrigerator for up to 5 days.

**TIP** Lentils will absorb the flavor of whatever they're cooked in, so substituting 1 cup of chicken broth for 1 cup of water will make this even tastier.

Per ¼ cup serving: Calories: 75; Protein: 6g; Fat: 1g; Carbs: 13g

# MILLET

PREP TIME: 1 MINUTE / COOK TIME: 20 MINUTES

*Millet is another protein-rich grain that also has a high-fat content, making it a really good alternative protein source.* **MAKES 2 CUPS**

**1 cup millet**

**2 cups water**

1. Place a small saucepan over medium heat, add the millet, and toast, stirring occasionally, until it is golden brown, about 5 minutes.

2. Stir in the water and increase the heat to high. Bring the mixture to a boil, then reduce the heat to low, cover, and simmer until tender, about 15 minutes.

3. Remove the saucepan from the heat and let stand for 10 minutes.

4. Fluff the millet with a fork and let cool.

5. Serve.

6. Store leftovers in an airtight container in the refrigerator for up to 5 days.

**TIP** Millet can be eaten as a breakfast cereal, too, like oatmeal. Top the grain with a pinch of salt, a slice of butter, a little milk, and some fresh fruit.

Per ¼ cup serving: Calories: 80; Protein: 3g; Fat: 1g; Carbs: 15g

# SWEET POTATOES

PREP TIME: 5 MINUTES / COOK TIME: 35 MINUTES

*Sweet potatoes are an excellent addition to any meal or a tremendously flavorful, nutritious addition to store-bought food.* **MAKES 2 CUPS**

**2 sweet potatoes, scrubbed
and halved lengthwise**

1. Preheat the oven to 400°F. Line a baking sheet with parchment paper or aluminum foil.

2. Place the sweet potatoes, cut-side up, on the baking sheet. Bake until tender, 25 to 35 minutes.

3. Cool the potatoes, then cut them into bite-size chunks.

4. Serve.

5. Store leftovers in an airtight container in the refrigerator for up to 3 days.

> **TIP** You can also mash the roasted sweet potato, depending on the meal you are adding this tasty addition to and the size of your dog.

Per ¼ cup serving: Calories: 34; Protein: 1g; Fat: 0g; Carbs: 8g

# SCRAMBLED EGGS

PREP TIME: 2 MINUTES / COOK TIME: 5 MINUTES

*Scrambled eggs are a great source of protein, and they help keep your dog's coat shiny.* **SERVES 1**

**1 large egg**

**1 tablespoon unsalted butter**

1. Whisk the egg in a small bowl.

2. Heat the butter in a small skillet over medium-low heat.

3. Add the beaten egg to the skillet and scramble, pulling the egg toward you and folding it, until it forms soft curds and there is no liquid left in the skillet.

4. Cool the egg and serve.

**TIP** Since you aren't whisking any milk or seasoning into the egg, you can mix the egg directly in the skillet.

Per serving: Calories: 174; Protein: 6g; Fat: 16g; Carbs: 0g

# MASHED BUTTERNUT SQUASH

PREP TIME: 20 MINUTES / COOK TIME: 30 MINUTES

*Squash come in many different sizes, with long and short necks and varying bases. Depending on the size of your squash, you will generally get between 1 and 3 cups of mash from a medium squash.*

**MAKES 1 TO 3 CUPS**

1 medium butternut
  squash, peeled, seeded,
  and chopped

2 tablespoons olive oil

1. Preheat the oven to 400°F. Line a baking sheet with parchment paper or aluminum foil.

2. In a large bowl, toss together the squash and olive oil. Spread the butternut squash on the prepared baking sheet.

3. Roast the squash for 30 minutes, or until golden brown.

4. Transfer the squash to the large bowl and mash with a potato masher.

5. Let the squash cool before serving.

6. Store leftovers in an airtight container in the refrigerator or portioned into sealed plastic bags for up to 4 days or in the freezer for 3 months.

**TIP** This dish is another great use for the immersion blender with a whisk attachment. This tool will make quick work of your roasted butternut squash. You can also leave the squash in cubes depending on the dish you are serving.

Per ¼ cup serving: Calories: 41; Protein: <1g; Fat: 2g; Carbs: 5g

# ROASTED BROCCOLI

*Broccoli, when chopped and cooked, is an excellent source of iron and vitamin C. Be sure to use only the florets—the stalks can present a choking hazard.* **MAKES 2 CUPS**

**6 ounces broccoli florets**
**2 tablespoons olive oil**

1. Preheat the oven to 450°F. Line a baking sheet with parchment paper or aluminum foil.

2. In a large bowl, toss together the broccoli and olive oil. Spread the broccoli on the prepared baking sheet.

3. Roast the broccoli for 20 minutes, until browned.

4. Let the broccoli cool before serving.

5. Store leftovers in an airtight container or portioned into sealed plastic bags in the refrigerator for up to 4 days or in the freezer for 3 months.

> **TIP** This is a delicious and easy way to prepare broccoli. If you're not making it for the dogs, add some sea salt when you toss the florets with the oil.

---

Per ¼ cup serving: Calories: 38; Protein: <1g; Fat: 4g; Carbs: 1g

# MASHED CAULIFLOWER

PREP TIME: 5 MINUTES / COOK TIME: 15 MINUTES

*Cauliflower is used a great deal these days in place of regular potatoes because when mashed, this cruciferous vegetable is fluffy and almost indistinguishable from the regular mash. Your dogs will love it!* **MAKES 2 CUPS**

2 cups water

1 large head
  cauliflower, chopped

1 tablespoon
  unsalted butter

1. Bring the water to a boil over medium-high heat in a medium saucepan fitted with a steamer basket. Add the cauliflower, cover, and steam for about 15 minutes, or until tender.

2. Carefully remove the steamer basket from the pot and transfer the cauliflower to a large bowl.

3. Add the butter and, using an immersion blender, purée the cauliflower into a mash.

4. Store leftovers in an airtight container or portioned into sealed plastic bags in the refrigerator for up to 4 days or in the freezer for 3 months.

**TIP** Cauliflower can be very messy to chop; for some reason, little bits seem to fly everywhere. A food processor can help you achieve a mess-free preparation.

Per ¼ cup serving: Calories: 39; Protein: 2g; Fat: 2g; Carbs: 6g

# ASPARAGUS AND HARDBOILED EGG

PREP TIME: 5 MINUTES / COOK TIME: 10 MINUTES

*Asparagus delivers vitamins A, C, E, and K, as well as fiber, folic acid, and chromium, a necessary trace mineral. Add a protein-packed egg to make a perfect snack.* **MAKES 2 TO 3 CUPS**

1 large egg

2 cups water

1 pound asparagus, trimmed and chopped

1. Fill a small saucepan two-thirds full of water and bring to a boil over high heat.

2. Use a spoon or ladle to place the egg into the boiling water and boil for 10 minutes.

3. Meanwhile, bring the 2 cups of water to a boil over medium-high heat in a medium saucepan fitted with a steamer basket. Add the asparagus, cover, and steam for about 10 minutes, or until tender. Transfer the asparagus to a medium bowl.

4. Carefully remove the egg from the boiling water and place it in a bowl. Run cool water over it for a few minutes.

5. Peel and slice the cooled egg and mix it with the asparagus.

6. Let the mixture cool before serving.

7. Store leftovers in an airtight container or portioned into sealed plastic bags in the refrigerator for up to 4 days or in the freezer for 3 months.

**TIP** This is a great treat to have on hand, served warm or cold. Hardboiled eggs are something I keep in my refrigerator all the time because they are so versatile.

Per ¼ cup serving: Calories: 22; Protein: 2g; Fat: 1g; Carbs: 3g

# SAUTÉED ZUCCHINI

PREP TIME: 5 MINUTES / COOK TIME: 10 MINUTES

*Zucchini is jam packed with minerals—calcium, iron, magnesium, phosphorus, and potassium—plus vitamins A, B (folic acid), C, E, and K.*

**MAKES 2 CUPS**

2 zucchini, chopped
2 tablespoons olive oil

1. Heat the oil in a large skillet over medium heat.

2. Add the zucchini and sauté, stirring often, for about 10 minutes, making sure all the pieces are crisp.

3. Let the zucchini cool before serving.

4. Store leftovers in an airtight container or portioned into sealed plastic bags in the refrigerator for up to 4 days or in the freezer for 3 months.

**TIP** Add a hardboiled egg to your zucchini to make a perfect snack for your dog. Rotating the type of green vegetable with the egg adds variety to your pet's diet.

Per ¼ cup serving: Calories: 38; Protein: 1g; Fat: 4g; Carbs: 2g

# ROASTED BEETS

PREP TIME: 15 MINUTES / COOK TIME: 40 MINUTES

*Beetroots bring iron, fiber, manganese, potassium, and vitamins B9 and C to your dog's dish, and they play a role in improved blood circulation.* **MAKES 2 CUPS**

4 medium beets, peeled        1 tablespoon olive oil
  and chopped

1. Preheat the oven to 400°F. Line a baking sheet with parchment paper or aluminum foil.

2. In a large bowl, toss together the beets and olive oil. Arrange the beets on the baking sheet.

3. Roast, turning occasionally, until tender, 30 to 40 minutes.

4. Let the beets cool before serving.

5. Store leftovers in an airtight container or portioned into sealed plastic bags in the refrigerator for up to 4 days or in the freezer for 3 months.

**TIP** Don't be alarmed when cleaning up after your dogs after they've eaten beets—their stool will be red. It's nothing to worry about. That's just the pigment called betanin that hasn't broken down completely.

Per ¼ cup serving: Calories: 33; Protein: 1g; Fat: 2g; Carbs: 4g

## Chapter Seven

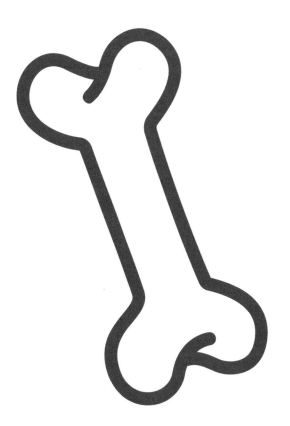

Some of these recipes will take some time, so plan ahead. They are such a great source of nutrients and so cost-friendly that they are a must-have in your dog-food-making plan! An all-time favorite of mine, and my dogs, is bone broth. You can ask your local butcher for beef, lamb, or chicken bones and get them at little to no cost. All the butchers I have met have been happy to give this stuff away. Simmering the bones in water for a long time will break down all the nutrients and create an incredibly healthy finished broth, which will last a long time in the freezer. Use the broth immediately or cool and store it as quickly as possible, because broth can start to form bacteria between 40°F and 140°F.

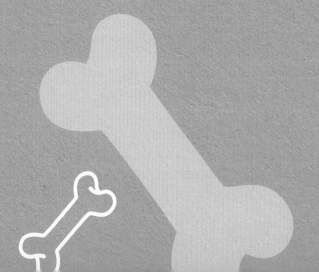

# BEEF BONE BROTH

PREP TIME: 15 MINUTES / COOK TIME: 11 TO 13 HOURS

*Beef bone broth is a hearty, thick, and flavorful stock. The marrow adds a rich flavor and a single batch of broth can enhance many meals.* **MAKES 10 CUPS**

3 pounds beef bones (ribs, marrow, knuckles, and any other bones)

10 celery stalks, cut into 1-inch pieces

4 carrots, peeled and cut into 1-inch pieces

1 tablespoon apple cider vinegar

1. Preheat the oven to 450°F.

2. Place the bones in a large roasting pan and roast for 1 hour, turning with tongs after 30 minutes.

3. Transfer the bones to a large stockpot and add the celery, carrots, and apple cider vinegar. Add enough water to cover the bones by about 3 inches.

4. Place the stockpot over high heat and bring to a boil. Reduce the heat to low, cover, and simmer gently for 10 to 12 hours.

5. Cool the stock for 30 minutes, then use tongs to remove the larger bones. Strain the stock into a large bowl and discard the leftover vegetables and bones.

6. Pour the broth into clean jars or containers and let cool. Seal the jars and refrigerate for up to 5 days or freeze for up to 2 months.

**TIP** After straining the broth, carefully remove the bones and scrape any marrow back into the pot. There is so much good stuff in the marrow, including more flavor.

Per 1 cup serving: Calories: 64; Protein: 6g; Fat: 4g; Carbs: 1g

# LAMB BONE BROTH

PREP TIME: 15 MINUTES / COOK TIME: 11 TO 13 HOURS

*Bone broth has cartilage, which contains glucosamine and chondroitin. These compounds have been proven to help reduce joint pain.* **MAKES 10 CUPS**

3 pounds lamb bones (ribs, marrow, knuckles, and any other bones)

10 celery stalks, cut into 1-inch pieces

4 carrots, peeled and cut into 1-inch pieces

1 tablespoon apple cider vinegar

1. Preheat the oven to 450°F.

2. Place the bones in a large roasting pan and roast for 1 hour, turning with tongs after 30 minutes.

3. Transfer the bones to a large stockpot and add the celery, carrots, and apple cider vinegar. Add enough water to cover the bones by about 3 inches.

4. Place the stockpot over high heat and bring to a boil. Reduce the heat to low, cover, and simmer gently for 10 to 12 hours.

5. Cool the stock for 30 minutes, then use tongs to remove the larger bones. Strain the stock into a large bowl and discard the leftover vegetables and bones.

6. Pour the broth into clean jars or containers and let cool. Seal the jars and refrigerate for up to 5 days or freeze for up to 2 months.

**TIP** Knuckles, joints, feet, and marrow bones work the best for broth, so become friends with your local butcher for a ready supply of these products.

Per 1 cup serving: Calories: 51; Protein: 5g; Fat: 3g; Carbs: 1g

# CHICKEN BONE BROTH

PREP TIME: 15 MINUTES / COOK TIME: 8 HOURS

*Chicken broth is so amazingly easy to make, you really can't go wrong. If you toss a stripped rotisserie chicken carcass in a pot of boiling water for 8 hours, you'll get a nutrient-packed broth perfect for your dog.* **MAKES 10 CUPS**

1 tablespoon olive oil

10 celery stalks, cut into
  1-inch pieces

4 carrots, peeled and cut
  into 1-inch pieces

2 chicken carcasses

1.  Heat the oil in a large stockpot over medium-high heat. Add the celery and carrots and sauté until softened, 7 to 10 minutes.

2.  Place the carcasses in the stockpot and add enough water to cover the bones by about 3 inches.

3.  Increase the heat to high and bring to a boil. Reduce the heat to low, cover, and simmer gently for about 8 hours.

4.  Cool the stock for 30 minutes, then use tongs to remove the larger bones. Strain the stock into a large bowl and discard the leftover vegetables and bones.

5.  Pour the broth into clean jars or containers and let cool. Seal the jars and refrigerate for up to 5 days or freeze for up to 2 months.

> **TIP** Chicken feet are super cheap and contain a lot of gelatin, which is necessary for a stellar bone broth.

Per 1 cup serving: Calories: 69; Protein: 4g; Fat: 5g; Carbs: 1g

# VEGETABLE STOCK

PREP TIME: 15 MINUTES / COOK TIME: 2 HOURS

*Vegetable stock for dogs is a little plain; many ingredients that go into stock for humans, whether meat or vegetable, are not safe for dogs. When there are bones or meat, there is more of the color and flavor we're used to seeing in broth. This is still a healthy stock, packed with nutrients, vitamins, and minerals, so don't worry if it looks a little thin.* **MAKES 10 CUPS**

1 tablespoon olive oil

10 celery stalks, cut into
  1-inch pieces

4 carrots, peeled and cut
  into 1-inch pieces

6 cups cold water

1. Heat the oil in a large stockpot over medium-high heat. Add the celery and carrots and sauté until softened, 7 to 10 minutes.

2. Stir in the water, increase the heat to high, and bring to a boil.

3. Reduce the heat to low, cover, and simmer gently for about 2 hours.

4. Cool the stock for 30 minutes, then strain the stock into a large bowl and discard the leftover vegetables.

5. Pour the stock into clean jars or containers and let cool. Seal the jars and refrigerate for up to 5 days or freeze for up to 2 months.

**TIP** Vegetable stock can always be substituted for other stocks for a slightly lighter meal.

Per 1 cup serving: Calories: 13; Protein: <1g; Fat: 1g; Carbs: 1g

# TURKEY PAN GRAVY

PREP TIME: 2 MINUTES / COOK TIME: 15 MINUTES

*Simple pan gravy can be made using the fat and leftovers after cooking ground turkey. This method takes so little time and effort, you will wonder why you don't make gravy for everything!* **MAKES 1 TO 2 CUPS**

Drippings from cooking
  ground turkey

1 to 2 tablespoons flour
2 cups chicken broth

1. Place the skillet with the drippings over medium heat and whisk in the flour until the roux that forms is bubbly, about 5 minutes, taking care to scrape any bits from the bottom of the pan.

2. Whisk in the broth, ¼ cup at a time, until the desired amount of gravy and thickness is reached.

3. Simmer, whisking constantly, until the gravy is thick and fragrant, about 10 minutes.

4. Cool before serving.

5. Store leftovers in an airtight container in the refrigerator for up to 2 days.

**TIP** Leave a little extra fat in the skillet and put a bit of meat back in to bulk up the amount of gravy. Make enough for your dinner, and pour a little in the dog bowl, too.

Per 1 cup serving: Calories: 45; Protein: 3g; Fat: 1g; Carbs: 8g

# BEEF PAN GRAVY

PREP TIME: 2 MINUTES / COOK TIME: 15 MINUTES

*Who doesn't love gravy? Everything is better with sauce. Maybe we can't eat it every day, but it is undoubtedly delicious. Funny that something this yummy is scraped together from the bits at the bottom of the skillet. All the flavor left behind gets a new life with a little effort.* **MAKES 1 TO 2 CUPS**

Drippings from cooking
  ground beef or steak

1 to 2 tablespoons flour
2 cups beef broth

1. Place the skillet with the drippings over medium heat and whisk in the flour until the roux that forms is bubbly, about 5 minutes, taking care to scrape any bits from the bottom of the pan.

2. Whisk in the broth, ¼ cup at a time, until the desired amount of gravy and thickness is reached.

3. Simmer, whisking constantly, until the gravy is thick and fragrant, about 10 minutes.

4. Cool before serving.

5. Store leftovers in an airtight container in the refrigerator for up to 2 days.

> **TIP** If you have leftovers, be sure to heat this up on the stove top—bring it to a boil, let cool, then serve again.

Per 1 cup serving: Calories: 75; Protein: 7g; Fat: 2g; Carbs: 8g

# CHICKEN PAN GRAVY

PREP TIME: 2 MINUTES / COOK TIME: 15 MINUTES

*Pan gravies are so easy to make; they will thicken up right in front of you as you stir in the flour, like culinary magic.* **MAKES 1 TO 2 CUPS**

Drippings from cooking
  ground chicken, chicken
  breasts, or thighs

1 to 2 tablespoons flour
2 cups chicken broth

1. Place the skillet with the drippings over medium heat and whisk in the flour until the roux that forms is bubbly, about 5 minutes, taking care to scrape any bits from the bottom of the pan.

2. Whisk in the broth, ¼ cup at a time, until the desired amount of gravy and thickness is reached.

3. Simmer, whisking constantly, until the gravy is thick and fragrant, about 10 minutes.

4. Cool before serving.

5. Store leftovers in an airtight container in the refrigerator for up to 2 days.

**TIP** You can always add more broth or more flour to get the desired consistency.

Per 1 cup serving: Calories: 45; Protein: 3g; Fat: 1g; Carbs: 8g

# SARDINE AND ARROWROOT GRAVY

PREP TIME: 2 MINUTES / COOK TIME: 15 MINUTES

*If you're using sardines for anything and want to make some delicious fish gravy, use this simple gravy recipe. You will not get enough gravy for leftovers, just enough for a single tasty meal topping.* **MAKES ½ CUP**

Oil from 1 (4-ounce) tin sardines

1 to 2 tablespoons arrowroot flour

¼ to ½ cup broth, as needed

1. Pour the sardine oil into a small saucepan over medium-high heat and bring to a boil.

2. Reduce the heat to low, and stir in up to 2 tablespoons of arrowroot flour, and cook, whisking constantly, until the gravy thickens, about 15 minutes.

3. If the gravy is too thick, whisk in the broth, a couple of tablespoons at a time, until you reach the desired consistency.

4. Cool before serving.

> **TIP** Sardine gravy is high in fatty acids that are great for the joints, skin, heart, brain activity, and more.

Per ¼ cup serving: Calories: 76; Protein: <1g; Fat: 7g; Carbs: 4g

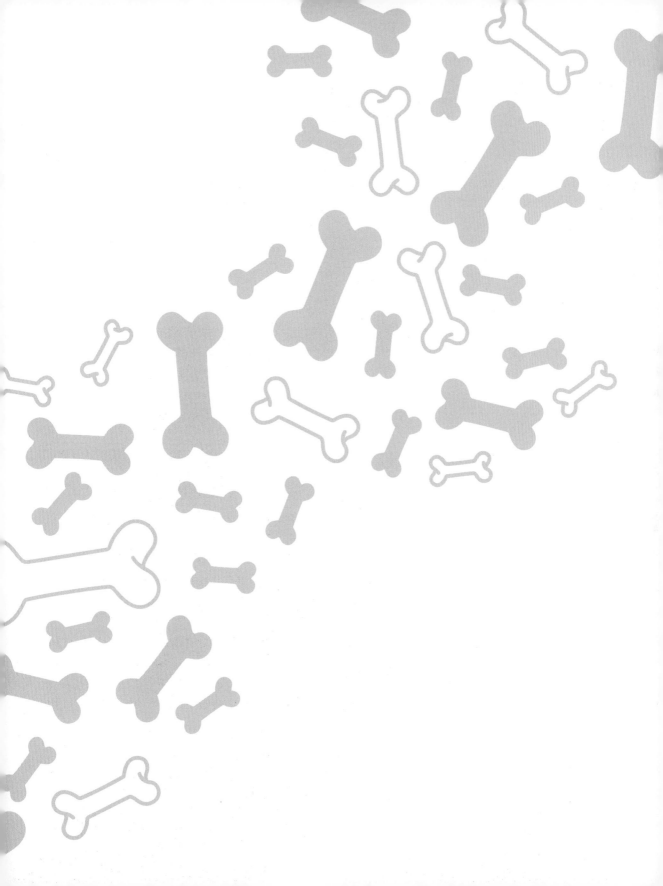

## Chapter Eight

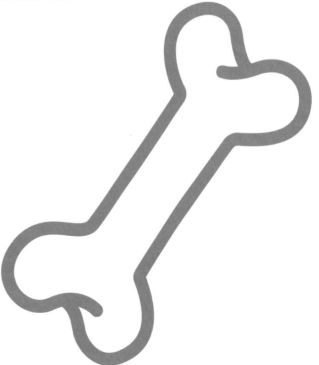

Since you are making a meal for your dog anyway, why not double the recipe and create something delicious for you as well? Pick a recipe from anywhere in this book—any choice will do because they all taste fabulous, if you ask me—double it, and then split it in half, people portion and dog portion. This chapter gives you some ideas for other meals that you can share with your pup. You will be leaving the dog's meal as is, except maybe putting it through a food processor if your buddy is small or has a problem with large pieces of food. The people portion can be spiced to suit your palate and arranged attractively on a beautiful plate. For example, if you're making a fried rice meal, add soy sauce to yours along with salt, pepper, hot sauce, onions, garlic, or anything else your dog should not eat. By sharing the recipe, the bulk of your work is done, and you will share a fun bonding moment with your dog eating the same meal.

# TUNA NOODLE WITH CHEESY VEGGIES

PREP TIME: 5 MINUTES / COOK TIME: 20 MINUTES

*The beauty of making human-grade food for your pets is how easy it is to share your meals with them! Rice is a diet staple for both me and my dogs, and by separating out my hounds' portion early in the process, I can add cheese and seasoning to my helping without worrying about their sensitive stomachs.* **MAKES 10 CUPS**

1 (16-ounce) package
  egg noodles
2 cups water
8 ounces frozen peas
  and carrots

1 (5-ounce) can
  water-packed tuna
Shredded sharp Cheddar
  cheese, for people portion
Sea salt, for people portion

Freshly ground black
  pepper, for people portion

1. Cook the egg noodles according to the package instructions, or uncovered on high for 6 to 8 minutes.

2. Meanwhile, bring the water to a boil in a medium saucepan fitted with a steamer basket. Add the peas and carrots, cover, and steam for about 10 minutes, or until tender.

3. Using a food processor, purée the cooked peas and carrots.

4. Transfer the noodles to a large bowl, add the puréed vegetables and tuna with its liquid, and mix together well.

5. For the dog portion, transfer half into a separate bowl. Let cool before serving.

6. For the people portion, add cheese, stirring to combine. Season with salt and pepper and serve.

7. Store leftovers in an airtight container or portioned into sealed plastic bags in the refrigerator for up to 4 days or in the freezer for 3 months.

**TIP** Remember to be aware of your dog's temperament. Dogs can become aggressive over food. Even a very well-behaved pet has the capacity to act like a wild animal when a delicious meal is placed in front of them.

Per 1 cup serving (10 per recipe): Calories: 204; Protein: 10g; Fat: 3g; Carbs: 35g

# CHEESY CHICKEN AND BROCCOLI BAKE

PREP TIME: 10 MINUTES / COOK TIME: 45 MINUTES

*Chicken and broccoli swimming in a melted cheese sauce make this meal a hearty way to fill up. Although delicious, the cheese sauce is just for us; it is just too much dairy for the pups.* **MAKES 10 CUPS**

6 cups water, divided

2 cups white rice

1 cup small broccoli florets

1 pound frozen skinless boneless chicken breasts

12 slices 2% American cheese, cut into ¼-by-¼-inch squares, for people portion

½ to 1 cup 2% milk, divided, for people portion

1 tablespoon yellow mustard, for people portion

Freshly ground black pepper, for people portion

2 tablespoons pumpkin purée

1.  Place 4 cups of water and the rice in a large saucepan over medium-high heat and bring to a boil. Reduce the heat to low, cover, and simmer until the rice is tender and the water is absorbed, about 20 minutes.

2.  Meanwhile, bring the remaining 2 cups of water to a boil in a medium saucepan fitted with a steamer basket. Add the broccoli, cover, and steam for about 10 minutes, or until tender.

3.  Fill a large stockpot about two-thirds full of water and bring to a boil over high heat. Add the chicken breasts, then reduce the heat to medium and simmer until the chicken is cooked through, 15 to 25 minutes.

4.  Heat the cheese in a small nonstick saucepan over low heat. Whisk in ½ cup of milk and the yellow mustard. Season with black pepper.

5.  Cook, stirring occasionally, until the cheese is melted, and the sauce is creamy, adding more milk if desired, about 10 minutes.

6.  Cut the cooked chicken into bite-size cubes.

7.  For the dog portion, mix together the chicken, broccoli, rice, and pumpkin purée in a medium bowl. Let cool before serving.

8. For the people portion, place the chicken and broccoli in a casserole and cover in cheese sauce. Place the casserole on the middle rack in the oven, and set to low broil for 5 to 10 minutes, or until slightly golden brown on top.

9. Store leftovers in an airtight container or portioned into sealed plastic bags in the refrigerator for up to 4 days or in the freezer for 3 months.

> **TIP** Make sure you're familiar with any food aggressions your dog may have before eating together, and, of course, don't share a plate!

---

Per 1 cup serving for dog portion: Calories: 184; Protein: 12g; Fat: 1g; Carbs: 31g

Per 1 cup serving for people portion: Calories: 264; Protein: 18g; Fat: 6g; Carbs: 31g

# SHRIMP WITH GREENS AND RICE

PREP TIME: 15 MINUTES / COOK TIME: 30 MINUTES

*Shrimp is brain food for all kinds of species. Enjoy yours with some wine, but make sure not to share!* **MAKES 6 CUPS**

6 cups water, divided

2 cups white rice

1 cup chopped green beans
  (about 2-inch pieces)

2 cups kale

2 tablespoons unsalted
  butter, divided

8 ounces frozen peeled and
  deveined shrimp, thawed
  and tails removed

1. Place 4 cups of water and the rice in a large saucepan over medium-high heat and bring to a boil. Reduce the heat to low, cover, and simmer until the rice is tender and the water is absorbed, about 20 minutes.

2. Meanwhile, bring the remaining 2 cups of water to a boil in a medium saucepan fitted with a steamer basket. Add the green beans, cover, and steam for about 10 minutes, or until tender.

3. Melt 1 tablespoon of butter in a medium skillet over medium-high heat. Add the shrimp and sauté until they are cooked through, about 5 minutes. Remove the shrimp from the pan, set aside, and keep warm. Melt the other tablespoon of butter in the skillet over medium-high heat, and add 2 cups of kale. Sauté, covered, for about 5 minutes, then remove the lid, and continue to cook for about 5 more minutes, until the moisture has evaporated.

4. For the dog portion, chop half the shrimp and mix it together with the green beans and rice. Let the mixture cool before serving.

5. For the people portion, combine the kale and rice in a serving bowl. Add whole cooked shrimp on top and serve.

6. Store leftovers in an airtight container or portioned into sealed plastic bags in the refrigerator for up to 4 days or in the freezer for 3 months.

**FUN FACT** Flamingos are pink because of their diet of brine shrimp, algae, and crustaceans, but don't get too excited—it takes way more shrimp than your pup will eat to turn them pink.

Per 1 cup serving (6 per recipe): Calories: 384; Protein: 30g; Fat: 6g; Carbs: 54g

# QUINOA AND SALMON

PREP TIME: 20 MINUTES / COOK TIME: 45 MINUTES

*So much good stuff is packed into salmon! Here's your chance to not feel guilty about taking the fleshiest piece for yourself while still letting your pup have a fatty, nutrient-filled feast. Think of it as a favor!* **MAKES 10 CUPS**

| | | |
|---|---|---|
| 2 cups water | 8 ounces boneless | 2 cups chopped cucumber |
| 1 cup quinoa | salmon fillets | 1 cup chopped apples |

1. Place the water and the quinoa in a large saucepan over medium-high heat. Bring to a boil, then reduce the heat to low and simmer until tender, about 15 minutes. Remove the saucepan from the heat and let stand 5 minutes.

2. Meanwhile, preheat the oven to 400°F.

3. Place a 12-inch piece of aluminum foil on a work surface and place the salmon fillet in the center. Cover the fish with the cucumber and apples and fold the edges of the foil up to form a sealed packet.

4. Place the packet in a small baking dish and bake until the salmon is cooked through, 10 to 15 minutes.

5. Remove the packet from the oven.

6. For the dog portion, in a medium bowl, mix together half of the salmon, cucumber, apples, and quinoa, breaking up or flaking the salmon as you go. Let cool before serving.

7. For the people portion, in a medium bowl, stir together the remaining half of the quinoa, cucumber, and apples, top with a salmon fillet, and serve.

8. Store leftovers in an airtight container or portioned into sealed plastic bags in the refrigerator for up to 4 days or in the freezer for 3 months.

**TIP** Crumble some nori over the top for added flavor.

Per 1 cup serving (6 per recipe): Calories: 175; Protein: 12g; Fat: 3g; Carbs: 25g

# CHICKEN WITH SUMMER SQUASH

PREP TIME: 10 MINUTES / COOK TIME: 20 MINUTES

*Squash is loaded with vitamins A, B$_6$, and C plus lots of good fiber, folate, magnesium, phosphorus, potassium, and riboflavin. Bake it or boil it for an easy add-on to your dog's dish.* **MAKES 10 CUPS**

4 cups water

2 cups white rice

1 pound skinless boneless
  chicken breast

1 tablespoon olive oil

2 cups chopped
  summer squash

1 cup chopped cauliflower

Sea salt, for people portion

Freshly ground black pepper,
  for people portion

1. Place the water and rice in a large saucepan over medium-high heat and bring to a boil. Reduce the heat to low, cover, and simmer until the rice is tender and the liquid is absorbed, about 20 minutes.

2. Meanwhile, heat the oil in a large skillet over medium heat. Add the chicken breast and sauté for about 3 minutes on each side, until the chicken is cooked through (165°F).

3. Reduce the heat to medium and stir in the summer squash and cauliflower. Cook, stirring occasionally, for 6 to 7 minutes, until the vegetables are tender and browned.

4. In a large bowl, combine the rice, cauliflower, and summer squash.

5. For the dog's portion, chop the chicken into bite-size pieces, add it to a portion of the rice and veggies, let cool, and serve.

6. For the people portion, serve the rice with veggies in a bowl, top with sliced chicken, and season with salt and pepper.

**TIP** You can swap in almost any color squash that's in season, or create a colorful mélange.

Per 1 cup serving (10 per recipe): Calories: 199; Protein: 12g; Fat: 3g; Carbs: 32g

# SIMPLE BEEF STEW

PREP TIME: 30 MINUTES / COOK TIME: 1 HOUR

*I love beef stew. As soon as the weather gets a little chilly, and the leaves start to change color, the smell of this stew coming from the kitchen just seems to complete the season. Note that diced tomatoes **are not** safe for the dogs. This is a for-people-only ingredient.*

**MAKES 12 CUPS**

1 (24-ounce) package no-salt-added beef broth

2 russet potatoes, peeled and cut into 1-inch cubes

3 tablespoons olive oil, divided

2 pounds round beef steak or chuck, cut into 1-inch pieces, divided

2 cups chopped carrots

2 cups chopped celery

1 (28-ounce) can diced tomatoes, for people portion

Sea salt, for people portion

Freshly ground black pepper, for people portion

1. In a large stockpot over high heat, combine the broth and potatoes and bring to a boil. Reduce the heat to low, cover, and simmer for 15 minutes, or until tender.

2. Meanwhile, heat 1 tablespoon of oil in a large saucepan over medium-high heat. Add half the beef and sauté until it is browned, 5 to 10 minutes. Transfer the beef to a plate using a slotted spoon and set aside. Repeat this process using 1 tablespoon of oil and the remaining half of beef.

3. Add the remaining 1 tablespoon of oil to the saucepan, still over medium-high heat. Add the carrots and celery and sauté until they are tender, about 5 minutes.

4. Transfer the beef and vegetables to the stockpot with the broth and potatoes and simmer for 15 minutes.

CONTINUED

5.  For the dog portion, transfer half of the stew to a medium bowl. Let cool before serving.

6.  For the people portion, stir the diced tomatoes into the remaining half of stew in the stockpot. Season with salt and pepper and serve.

7.  Store leftovers in an airtight container or portioned into sealed plastic bags in the refrigerator for up to 4 days or in the freezer for 3 months.

**TIP** When cooking a meal for both you and your dogs, make sure not to include any for-people-only ingredients in their portions. When in doubt, leave it out.

Per 1 cup serving for dog portion: Calories: 173; Protein: 19g; Fat: 7g; Carbs: 9g

Per 1 cup serving for people portion: Calories: 187; Protein: 20g; Fat: 7g; Carbs: 12g

# CHICKEN WITH QUINOA AND SPINACH

PREP TIME: 15 MINUTES / COOK TIME: 45 MINUTES

*When I'm making a meal for my human family and my dogs at once, I'll usually get a little more extravagant (or, you know, use an extra pot or two). Think of it as an excuse to add a little extra oomph to both species' meals.* **MAKES 10 CUPS**

4 cups water

2 cups quinoa

1 pound frozen skinless
  boneless chicken

2 tablespoons olive oil

1 cup chopped
  summer squash

2 cups baby spinach

Soy sauce, for people
  portion

1. Place the water and the quinoa in a large saucepan over medium-high heat. Bring to a boil, then reduce the heat to low and simmer until tender, about 15 minutes. Remove the saucepan from the heat and let stand 5 minutes.

2. Meanwhile, fill a large stockpot over high heat about two-thirds full of water and bring to a boil. Add the chicken, then reduce the heat to medium and simmer until the chicken is cooked through, 15 to 25 minutes.

3. Heat the olive oil in a large skillet over medium-high heat. Add the summer squash and spinach and sauté until they are tender, 6 to 8 minutes. Remove the skillet from the heat.

4. Cut half the chicken into bite-size pieces for the dog portion and cut half into slices for yourself.

5. For the people portion, fill a serving bowl with quinoa, then top with the sliced chicken and vegetables. Drizzle with soy sauce and serve.

6. For the dog portion, in a medium bowl, mix together the quinoa, the bite-size pieces of chicken, and the vegetables. Let cool before serving.

7. Store leftovers in an airtight container or portioned into sealed plastic bags in the refrigerator for up to 4 days or in the freezer for 3 months.

**TIP** Be sure you always separate your dog's portion before you add any seasonings to your own.

Per 1 cup serving (10 per recipe): Calories: 211; Protein: 14g; Fat: 6g; Carbs: 26g

# HAMBURGERONI

PREP TIME: 15 MINUTES / COOK TIME: 45 MINUTES

*Perfect for a night when all your entire family wants to do is curl up by the fire. Make some cornbread to go with it for the humans.*

**MAKES 12 CUPS**

16 ounces dried macaroni

1 zucchini, chopped

1 cup peas

2 pounds ground beef

2 (28-ounce) cans diced tomatoes, for people portion

Sea salt, for people portion

Freshly ground black pepper, for people portion

Parmesan cheese, for people portion

1. Bring a large pot of water to a boil over high heat. Add the macaroni and cook until al dente, about 8 minutes. Drain the pasta and set aside.

2. Meanwhile, bring water to a boil in a medium saucepan fitted with a steamer basket. Add the zucchini and peas, cover, and steam for about 10 minutes, or until tender.

3. Heat a large skillet over medium-high heat. Add the beef and sauté until it is cooked through and browned, about 10 minutes.

4. Remove the beef from the heat and drain the excess fat from the skillet.

5. For the dog portion, transfer half of the beef to a large bowl. Add half the macaroni and half the steamed vegetables, stirring to combine. Let cool before serving.

6. For the people portion, add the diced tomatoes to the skillet with the remaining half of the beef. Add the remaining half of the vegetables. Season with salt and pepper and bring the sauce to a boil over medium-high heat. Reduce the heat to low and simmer for 30 minutes.

7. Place the remaining half of the macaroni in a serving bowl, then top with sauce and sprinkle with Parmesan cheese. Serve hot.

**TIP** You can get creative and add in anything you like to the sauce for the people portion. I like to add fresh mushrooms, black olives, and some fresh basil leaves.

Per 1 cup serving for dog portion: Calories: 345; Protein: 19g; Fat: 16g; Carbs: 30g

Per 1 cup serving for people portion: Calories: 375; Protein: 20g; Fat: 16g; Carbs: 37g

# MEASUREMENT CONVERSIONS

| | U.S. STANDARD | U.S. STANDARD (OUNCES) | METRIC (APPROXIMATE) |
|---|---|---|---|
| **VOLUME EQUIVALENTS (LIQUID)** | 2 tablespoons | 1 fl. oz. | 30 mL |
| | ¼ cup | 2 fl. oz. | 60 mL |
| | ½ cup | 4 fl. oz. | 120 mL |
| | 1 cup | 8 fl. oz. | 240 mL |
| | 1½ cups | 12 fl. oz. | 355 mL |
| | 2 cups or 1 pint | 16 fl. oz. | 475 mL |
| | 4 cups or 1 quart | 32 fl. oz. | 1 L |
| | 1 gallon | 128 fl. oz. | 4 L |
| **VOLUME EQUIVALENTS (DRY)** | ⅛ teaspoon | ———— | 0.5 mL |
| | ¼ teaspoon | ———— | 1 mL |
| | ½ teaspoon | ———— | 2 mL |
| | ¾ teaspoon | ———— | 4 mL |
| | 1 teaspoon | ———— | 5 mL |
| | 1 tablespoon | ———— | 15 mL |
| | ¼ cup | ———— | 59 mL |
| | ⅓ cup | ———— | 79 mL |
| | ½ cup | ———— | 118 mL |
| | ⅔ cup | ———— | 156 mL |
| | ¾ cup | ———— | 177 mL |
| | 1 cup | ———— | 235 mL |
| | 2 cups or 1 pint | ———— | 475 mL |
| | 3 cups | ———— | 700 mL |
| | 4 cups or 1 quart | ———— | 1 L |
| | ½ gallon | ———— | 2 L |
| | 1 gallon | ———— | 4 L |
| **WEIGHT EQUIVALENTS** | ½ ounce | ———— | 15 g |
| | 1 ounce | ———— | 30 g |
| | 2 ounces | ———— | 60 g |
| | 4 ounces | ———— | 115 g |
| | 8 ounces | ———— | 225 g |
| | 12 ounces | ———— | 340 g |
| | 16 ounces or 1 pound | ———— | 455 g |

| | FAHRENHEIT (F) | CELSIUS (C) (APPROXIMATE) |
|---|---|---|
| **OVEN TEMPERATURES** | 250°F | 120°C |
| | 300°F | 150°C |
| | 325°F | 180°C |
| | 375°F | 190°C |
| | 400°F | 200°C |
| | 425°F | 220°C |
| | 450°F | 230°C |

# RESOURCES

American Kennel Club: AKC.org

American Society for the Prevention of Cruelty to Animals: ASPCA.org

Association of American Feed Control Officials: TalksPetFood.AAFCO.org

Center for Science in the Public Interest: CSPINET.org

The Dog Food Advisor: DogFoodAdvisor.com

Pet MD: PetMD.com

U.S. Food and Drug Administration: FDA.gov

# RECIPE INDEX

# INDEX

# ACKNOWLEDGMENTS

To Joni, Jackson, Jack, Zoe, Kim, Kees, Sadie, Diesel, Benny, Pumpkin, Meggie, Rupert, Leo, Sammi, Stealth, Sophie, Maddie, Roxy, Stinkerbell, Samson, Otis, Bumper, Shirley, Coco, Santino, Frankie, and the rest of my loyal crew: You are all very good buddies, and proof that love multiplies; you always have enough to go around.

And I'd like to thank my favorite humans, Dee, Morgan, Todd, Marissa, Eva, Paloma, Mom, Barry, Maegan, Margie, and Larry, for never making me feel guilty for saying, "Sorry I'm running late—I was cooking for the dogs."

# ABOUT THE AUTHOR

Los Angeles native **Scott Shanahan** has spent 15 years training, socializing, and caring for the canines of the rich and famous. As a frequent in-home caretaker for the dogs he worked with, Scott learned about the unique needs of his canine clients, many of whom were eating human-grade food or highly customized diets. He noticed the impact food was having on each animal's quality of life. His fascination with canine diet and the improved quality of life it provides has driven him to develop affordable, customizable dog food recipes that the non–rich-and-famous can make for their dogs at home. Today, Scott lives in a 250-square-foot tiny house with his wife, daughter, and three mismatched dogs whom he cooks for every night. You can find him on Instagram at @minimalish.house and see the anarchy for yourself.